School Public Relations:
Issues and Cases

School Public Relations:

Issues and Cases

JAMES J. JONES

Professor of Education, School of Education
University of Miami

and

IRVING W. STOUT

Dean, Graduate College
Arizona State University

1960

G. P. Putnam's Sons

NEW YORK

Preface

THE PURPOSE of this book is to identify and to treat some of the most common issues in American public education which affect school public relations. A related purpose is to illustrate, by means of carefully chosen cases, how certain schools have handled these issues. Each issue is followed by two cases which exemplify various ways in which it may be treated. These cases are real; they represent examples of effective and ineffective school public-relations practices in selected school systems throughout the United States. They are presented not as the only way to handle the issues discussed but as a means for the stimulation of thoughtful consideration and action. No doubt certain schools or school systems will need to face issues not mentioned here. Once an issue is discussed and thought about in the light of its effect on the public, far fewer mistakes are likely to be made concerning it.

The experience of the authors as public-school teachers, administrators, and university professors in graduate schools of education indicates that public relations are tied to every aspect of schoolwork and to many community contacts. It is almost impossible for one to name a phase of schoolwork which does not in some manner involve, either directly or indirectly, an element of public relations.

This book is written for all persons who are interested in school public relations. It is addressed primarily to administrators, supervisors, and teachers, with the intent that it will serve these groups as a reference for both pre-service and in-service training. School-board members and members of parent-teacher associations will find it helpful in their considerations of school policy and practices.

Acknowledgments

DURING the writing of this book, Dr. John R. Beery, Dean of the School of Education, University of Miami, gave constant encouragement. Professors Samuel Ersoff of the University of Miami, Philip G. Smith of the University of Tennessee, Arthur M. Jarman of the University of Virginia, and Paul W. Seagers of Indiana University each read portions of this book and made helpful suggestions.

The writers are indebted to the many superintendents, principals, supervisors, teachers, school-board members, and graduate students who aided them in the writing of cases.

Special thanks are extended to Isabella O. Klingler, Librarian, University of Miami Graduate School, who read the manuscript in its entirety and made suggestions. Also to James D. Lacey, advanced graduate student and instructor at the University of Miami, who proofread the manuscript, go our sincere thanks.

Finally, the authors are grateful to their wives, Mrs. Doris J. Jones and Mrs. Grace B. Stout, for their patience and understanding during the preparation of this book.

James J. Jones

Irving W. Stout

Contents

ix

3. Issues Dealing with Finance, Budget Preparation, and Control   44

4. Issues Dealing with the School Plant   71

5. Issues Dealing with Personnel Administration   91

6. Issues Dealing with Curriculum   113

IDENTIFICATION AND TREATMENT OF ISSUES AND CASES | 1.

Introduction

AN INVESTIGATION of the issues involved in school public relations raises many significant questions. What determines effective school-board membership? How does one distinguish between the functions of the school board and those of the superintendent? What local sources of revenue should be used to support public education? To what extent should the federal government aid public education? Should citizens take part in the planning of school plants? When should the school plant and facilities be used by outside groups? Should the merit salary schedule be used in the payment of teachers? To what extent are in-service educational programs effective? Should the faculty participate in policy development? What should be the scope of the educational program? Who should be the determiners of the curriculum? How should pupils be grouped for instruction? Is there value in homework for pupils? To what extent do parent-teacher associations promote school public relations? Should public opinion be given priority over professional opinion? Thirty such issues are treated in this book.

Increased Scope of School Public Relations

Not until recent years has much interest been manifested in studying the problems of school public relations. One may search in vain through the educational literature previous to the early 1920's for information concerning school public relations. Today, school administrators, professors of education, teachers, board members, and graduate students in education throughout the country are engaged to some extent in an effort to solve some of the problems involved in this area of administration, an area which cuts across all phases of education.

Although there has been a vast increase in the volume of research in school public relations, relatively few issues in the field have been completely or adequately resolved. It is doubtful if there has ever been a period in the history of American education when the need for public understanding and support of our public schools has been greater than now. So many changes in purposes, procedures, methods, size, and cost of schools have left the general public without adequate knowledge of the school and community. The complex society of today is in need of educational experiences considerably different from those which characterized the public schools a half century ago. As school personnel have attempted to formulate aims related to the preparation of children to meet the demands of this more complex society, they have found them difficult to express in simple terms, a factor which has resulted in yet more misunderstanding by the general public.

The positive progress of schools is reduced when patrons do not have adequate information about their schools. The American public is willing to accept the concept of change as applied to physical developments which affect their everyday living, such as the automatic defroster on refrigerators and the air conditioning in their homes, but they are not so quick to demand or to accept change in their social institutions. In far too many communities, education is a thing set apart from the public. As a result, one may find a tendency on the part of the public to leave things as they are, to oppose going along with those educators who attempt to point a way toward improvement of education.

Our American schools were taught for generations by persons who stepped aside from other activities to give their time to the training of children—persons whose main interest was not necessarily in the field of education. Although this is still true to some extent today, education has developed as a profession, and we have demanded increasingly higher standards of those who join its ranks. Patterns of administration and the structure of the school system have been revised in the light of research and experimentation. In this process the public has played a part, but often with hesitation and uncertainty.

Another need for school public relations is indicated by the fact that many of our school policies and some of our school statutes are the direct result of pressure groups and their influence on legislation. Not all pressure groups are bad, but many work for the vocal minority and do not represent the majority. It is well for the administrator to become aware of these groups which influence education, and it is imperative that professional people understand the nature of outside demands and pressures made on the public schools. Only after careful analysis of these demands can better school public relations be established.

The increased scope of public relations is reflected in the expansion of the branch of the National Education Association known as the National School Public Relations Association.

Although this organization has been in existence only since 1935, its publications and increasing services give witness to tremendous growth. Under the very capable leadership of Roy K. Wilson, the NSPRA has become a clearinghouse for ideas regarding school public relations. The organization has many publications to its credit, including a newsletter called *Trends,* a digest called *The School Bell,* and a weekly report entitled *Education U. S. A.*

The NSPRA holds periodic meetings in cooperation with the American Association of School Administrators and other national groups. It also conducts, each summer, a seminar on communications. Public-school systems and their employees would do well to consult the NSPRA and its staff for assistance in public relations.

It is almost impossible for the educator to have a relatively free hand in developing an enriched educational program if the public is left behind in its understanding of education. A well-planned program of school public relations is a necessity in a modern educational program. Administrators are beginning to realize that, in a democracy, the citizen will ultimately determine local policy with respect to education, and what parents think of their schools is conditioned by their knowledge of the schools' operation. It is imperative that the schools' public relations contribute to dissemination of that knowledge.

Nature of School Public Relations

A number of authorities have given their definitions of "public relations." The American Association of School Administrators' Twenty-eighth Yearbook states that "public relations seek to bring about a harmony of understanding between any group and the public it serves and upon whose good will it depends." [1] A school administrator who accepts this definition must be familiar with many areas of knowledge if he is to provide leadership for the proper interpretation of the school and community. Social and educational psychology, economics, sociology, history, and philosophy have contributions to make in this interpretation and should be understood by both the administration and the faculty.

Benjamin Fine, former education editor of the *New York Times,* sees public relations as having an even wider scope:

> Public relations is more than a narrow set of rules—it is a broad concept. It is the entire body of relationships that go to make our impressions of an individual, an organization, or an idea. In building good public relations, we must be aware of all the forces, drives, emotions, and conflicting and contradicting factors that are part of our social life and civilizations. [2]

A somewhat similar definition is given by Reeder, [3] who says public relations is that phase of school administration which seeks to bring a harmonious working relationship between the schools and the public which the schools serve.

The dividing line between the aspect of school administration known as "school public relations" and other aspects of school administration is extremely elusive. Every segment of the work of the schools, as well as the influence of the people of the community on the work of the schools, has some effect upon the working relationship of the schools and the community. School public relations is at work whether the faculty and staff are cognizant of it or not.

[1] American Association of School Administrators, *Public Relations for America's Schools,* The Association, Washington, D.C., 1950, p. 12.

[2] Benjamin Fine, *Educational Publicity,* Harper & Brothers, New York, 1943, p. 255.

[3] Ward G. Reeder, *An Introduction to Public School Relations,* The Macmillan Company, New York, 1953, p. 1.

In the present volume "school public relations" is used in an all-inclusive sense and denotes all the activities and relationships which exist in a two-way flow of ideas between school and community and which provide the basis for mutual understanding. "School public relations" and "public relations" will be used interchangeably with "school-community relations." The term "school public-relations program" is used to refer to a plan in which a variety of activities are organized and utilized to help develop better understanding and cooperation between school and community.

Modern Concepts of School Public Relations

In early American education the school was a source of community strength. Life was rather simple, and the general public understood most of what was taught in the schools. To be interested in and to share in education were accepted as responsibilities of the community almost without exception.

The American school system has developed largely as a local institution. So much control has remained with the community that, in many instances, small school districts have suffered severe handicaps in their attempts to operate school systems that were efficient. Despite these handicaps, however, progress has been made.

As public education became a state function, it began to veer away from so much attention to local ideas and beliefs.

> Public education became institutionalized when it became a state function. State laws determined the nature of the organization, the personnel, the program. Visiting committees were replaced by superintendents and principals, now clothed with official authority. . . . Boards of education began to draw away from the people who elected them.[4]

[4] William A. Yeager, *School-Community Relations,* The Dryden Press, Inc., New York, 1951, p. 104.

Four major concepts may be identified in regard to how school personnel feel about their relationships with the community. These concepts are indifference, school publicity, educational interpretation, and cooperative endeavor. It should not be concluded that these concepts are mutually exclusive. One may very well find an administrator who practices his public-relations program in such a manner as to involve two or more of these concepts.

Indifference

Some authorities have described this concept as the "hands-off" approach. "Indifference" was the attitude of many schoolmen, in the early part of the century, who felt that the schools belonged to the "professionals." Where this belief prevailed, administrators and teachers let it be known that the children were to be placed in the hands of those who knew best—the school personnel. The school program was to be designed by schoolmen and carried out by them. Parents were warned to accept without question the fact that professional people were in charge. Under this concept the home or the community had very little to say. Some schoolmen were indifferent to citizens who wanted to help with suggestions.

Where this concept prevails today, although there is naturally some contact between the school and the community, the school does what it desires and makes very little effort to give understandable data to parents and the public. The citizens, in turn, have a "let-alone" attitude toward their school.

School Publicity, or Selling the School to the Public

A second concept of school public relations has been called "school publicity," or "selling the school to the public."

The selling approach is largely one of telling the public,

combined with an attitude of "take our word for it." Some desirable techniques, however, have been developed under this approach. In an effort to secure quick results, some superintendents adopt a procedure which has proved successful in business—short but intensive publicity campaigns. This idea has much in its favor, but it also involves dangers which should be considered carefully by insightful school leaders and school boards.

Despite the fact that the school-publicity concept advocates continuous publicity, it fails to tell the full story of the activities of the schools. It is inadequate as a concept of school public relations because it implies that the public must be "sold" on what the schools are doing and it disregards the basic premise of public education, that is, that the public schools belong to the people. Under this concept the public is likely to be told only what the school wants to have known; the people are never sure that they receive all the data about the schools that they are entitled to have.

Educational Interpretation

Educational interpretation developed as a result of the recognition that the selling approach was not getting the job done. The concept implies that the schools must be interpreted to the community, but it makes no arrangements for a two-way communication between the school and the community. The direction and control of public relations and interpretation are the prerogatives of the professionals and the lay board of education. This approach involves an understanding of public opinion as a social force in the community and of social pressures and how to meet them, and it assumes that the public will accept the schools as they are presented and will be satisfied that the schools have done their best under existing laws and social and economic conditions. It takes more than constantly telling the public what the school is doing, however, to have a good public-relations program. Regardless of how well the public may be informed, the interpretation program must be based on an excellent school program; there must be a good school about which to tell the public.

Cooperative Endeavor

This concept of school public relations goes back to the early part of this century and considers the development and growth of the "whole child." It takes into consideration new discoveries concerning teaching and child development. It views the school as a social institution which should go forward as an integrated process. In order to accept this concept, one must recognize the two-way process—an understanding of the community by the school and an understanding of the school and its works by the community—and must also recognize that the school is but one social agency that works for the child. The home, the community, and the school should share their information relative to the total growth of the child. The cooperative direction of the three should be utilized to the fullest extent.

One of the ways in which school programs for public-school pupils may be improved is through the wholehearted cooperation of all who are concerned with their development, including the public, the profession, and the children. Enthusiastic and aggressive leadership should induce the selection of an advanced and satisfying concept that will help attain the goals which are sought for a given community. Although it is not likely that such a policy can be installed immediately, a good plan would be to begin at the level of community operation and to move to higher levels as fast as is thought advisable under existing conditions.

Purposes of School Public Relations

In an effective school public-relations program it is essential that those responsible for its development understand what the program seeks to accomplish. School public relations, like good teaching, must have well-defined purposes. The purposes of a school public-relations program are determined by the school's philosophy concerning the direction of school-community relations and the accepted principles underlying the program. A consensus of purposes of public-school relations by a number of authorities in educational administration is listed below:

1. To quicken the sense of responsibility in all citizens for thoughtful participation in school affairs.

2. To keep the people informed concerning the purposes, accomplishments, conditions, and needs of the school.

3. To show the public that they are really getting full value for their money.

4. To provide an agency whereby the public may identify and support the vital issues of education.

5. To develop an understanding of what is possible in education.

6. To build public confidence in the school system.

7. To develop and coordinate school activities with community activities in order to bring the school, the home, and the community closer together and to further American ideals of a good society.

8. To develop continuing public consciousness of the importance of the educational process in a democratic school organization.

9. To establish confidence in the functioning institution.

10. To improve the partnership concept through active parental participation.

John M. Hickey studied the public-relations programs of the schools of 83 cities of the United States and found eight objectives acceptable to more than 90 per cent of his respondents.

1. To inform the public as to the work of the school.

2. To establish confidence in the schools.

3. To rally support for proper maintenance of the educational program.

4. To develop awareness of the importance of education in a democracy.

5. To improve the partnership concept by uniting parents and teachers in meeting the educational needs of the children.

6. To integrate the home, the school, and the community in improving the educational opportunities for all children.

7. To evaluate the offerings of the schools in meeting the needs of the children of the community.

8. To correct misunderstandings as to the aims and activities of the school.[5]

Hickey's study dealt with 57 cities of over 100,000 population and 26 cities of less than 100,000 population. He did not attempt to discover what county school systems and schools in rural areas thought about these objectives. Although this study has certain limitations, it is perhaps the most thorough study of objectives made up to the present time. The purposes uncovered by Hickey are the ones most widely accepted today.

In order to help educate the public about its schools, there must be a continuous presentation of selected facts and pertinent information which show the school program in its true

[5] John M. Hickey, *The Direction of Public Relations in Cities of the United States,* unpublished doctor's dissertation, University of Pittsburgh, Pittsburgh, 1945.

light. No longer is the public-relations program of a school merely an attempt to sell the school in its best light to the public. Improvement of the school is one of the primary objectives of the good public-relations program; it calls for building understanding among adult members of the community so that they can intelligently evaluate the school program and its improvement. The public supports a cause in direct relation to its understanding of the cause.

Issues and Cases
Issue

An issue pertains to a debatable matter which usually has two or more sides and in which the correctness of no single viewpoint can be proved conclusively. It is often the subject matter of debate and controversy. An issue is more than a difficult problem. It is a matter which has provoked wide discussion, study, and thinking. The small and persistent problems of public-school systems are generally managed in such a way as not to be injurious to school public relations, but serious points of controversy will arouse the public. It is discipline, federal aid, and other such problems which do not have definite research answers that torment school administrators.

One purpose of this book is to identify controversial issues. The issues treated here have been identified through a thorough canvass of the available research in school public relations and educational administration, and they involve seven areas: school boards, finance and budget preparation, school plant, personnel policies, curriculum, instruction, and community groups.

Case

A case is a means of bringing into the classroom an honest report of a situation, for study by students and instructor. The case may be long or short, but it must be objective. It should be the type of case that promotes discussion and is capable of being interpreted.

The cases reported in this book represent actual situations which have been uncovered by the authors in various parts of the country. Some of these cases are written by individuals involved in the case, and all of them depict situations in which the board of education, the school superintendent or principal, teachers, citizens, pupils, and other administrators have been involved. The names of persons and places have been changed in each case. Immediately following the discussion of each issue, pro and con, two cases are presented, each of which shows a different approach to the issue. It is the hope of the authors that these cases and issues will furnish a springboard for class discussion which will provide further opportunity for learning about school public relations.

Selected Readings

American Association of School Administrators, *Public Relations for America's Schools,* Twenty-eighth Yearbook, The Association, Washington, D.C., 1950, Chap. I.

Andrews, M. G., "Pointers on Publicity," *Bulletin, National Association of Secondary School Principals,* **32**:160–170, February, 1948.

Fine, Benjamin, *Educational Publicity,* Harper & Brothers, New York, 1943, Chaps. IX, X.

Hagman, Harlan L., *A Study of the Theory and Some Present Practices in School Public Relations Administration,* unpublished doctor's dissertation, Northwestern University, Evanston, Ill., 1947.

Hickey, John M., *The Direction of Public Relations in Cities of the United States,* unpublished doctor's dissertation, University of Pittsburgh, Pittsburgh, 1945.

Jones, James J., "Modern Concepts of Public Relations," *Phi Delta Kappan,* **36:** 229–233, March, 1955.

Kindred, Leslie W., *School Public Relations,* Prentice-Hall, Inc., Englewood Cliffs, N.J., 1957, Chaps. I, II.

Langdon, Grace, and Stout, Irving W., *Helping Parents Understand Their Children,* Prentice-Hall, Inc., Englewood Cliffs, N.J., 1957, Chaps. III, IV.

National Society for the Study of Education, *Citizen Cooperation for Better Public Schools,* Fifty-third Yearbook of the NSSE, Pt. I, University of Chicago Press, Chicago, 1954.

Reeder, Ward G., *An Introduction to Public School Relations,* The Macmillan Company, New York, 1953, Chap. I.

Yeager, William A., *School-Community Relations,* The Dryden Press, Inc., New York, 1951, Chap. VI.

ISSUES DEALING WITH LOCAL SCHOOL BOARDS | 2.

A SCHOOL BOARD usually possesses powers assigned to it by constitutional and statutory law and has discretionary power extending beyond the limits of legal provisions. In most cases the board makes the ultimate financial decisions which determine the scope of educational service. It is almost impossible for a school system to maintain high levels of performance without a good board of education.

Through its work as a board and through the position of its members in the community, the school board occupies a strategic position in school public relations. The school board, as a body, may serve as a means of liaison between the school and the public, help formulate and adopt broad working policies, and provide for financing the community's educational needs. In addition, the board of education has a legal and moral responsibility to report to the public and to receive with understanding the reports and data from school administrative officers regarding the operation of the schools. The board should exchange information and ideas with the school executive, appraise public opinion, provide the means for interpretation, and help orient and educate new members.[1] The board should also use the professional staff in developing board policies for the school public-relations program.

The school's chief executive officer is the person charged with responsibility for the public-relations program. His task is to organize the machinery for school-community relationships toward unified operation. The superintendent is responsible to the board of education for all phases of the conduct of the schools. He should serve as a spokesman and an interpreter of the will of the board, and he should provide leadership toward a sound public-relations program. He should discover and analyze outside pressures and demands on the public schools, inform the board of education, help evaluate the educational program, and provide leadership and inspiration for the staff.

The ways in which local boards of education are selected, their size, their effectiveness, the division of labor between the board and the superintendent, how they evaluate the educational program, and their participation in state and national associations have much to do with helping communities decide whether their school systems deserve their good will and support.

How Should Local School-Board Members Be Selected?

Generally, in the United States, there are two methods for selecting school-board members. One is appointment by some governmental body; the other is election by popular vote. The power to determine what process shall be used is left to the legislature and not to the people of a local school district. Many well-qualified citizens who will accept an appointment to a public-school board well refuse to run for the position on

[1] See James J. Jones, "Some Activities and Responsibilities of School Boards in Public Relations," *Educational Administration and Supervision,* 39: 414–421, November, 1953.

an elective basis. Appointment is considered a high honor and a civic responsibility, although it usually does not carry a salary. Where school-board members are appointed, the appointing body is held responsible to the people. In the states that use the appointive method, appointment is usually made by mayors, judges, councils, or other public officals. When board members are appointed for long, overlapping terms after being nominated by representatives of civic or other organizations, there is less likelihood that they will be influenced by politics.

Procedures for the nomination of elected candidates range from organized caucuses to informal contacts with possible candidates. One major weakness of the election-by-popular-vote method is that no particular group is specified to be responsible for the nomination of candidates. A tenure of more than five years is desirable if a board member is to reach his maximum usefulness, and the length of service on the board tends to be greater under the appointive method than under the elective method. If board membership is continuously changing, the superintendent may have difficulty in working with new members, and the school program may suffer because of frequent changes in policies and practices. It has been suggested that the general public becomes more interested in its schools when school affairs are discussed during an election campaign, and that election of board members by popular vote permits the people to express themselves directly on school matters and gives the person elected a feeling of responsibility to those who elected him rather than to some city official. An appointed board, on the other hand, may feel that it owes allegiance to the appointing authority if a class of opinion occurs between the board and the appointing authority. An elected board should feel free to act independently, since its members are responsible to the general public. About 95 per cent of all local school-board members are now elected by popular vote, but the value of any method of selection will be determined, to a large extent, by the type of individual selected. It is possible to get good members by either election or appointment.

Case Number One illustrates how an appointed board member was influenced by his loyalty to the appointing body, at the cost of slighting his duties as a board member. The second case exemplifies an elected board member who also felt that his obligations were to those who helped put him in office rather than to the school system itself.

Case Number One—Mr. Brown

The setting for this case is an industrial area in a state which has its city board members appointed by the city councils. Mr. Brown, a new appointee, was a professional man who had grown up in the city and, in more recent years, had become well known for his ability to secure votes for his political party. He was sincere, intelligent, and desirous of helping the school board improve the public schools of his home town. He felt, however, a strong obligation to vote for whatever the mayor and city council felt was best for education. After all, he wanted to be loyal. An aggressive individual, he was elected chairman of the school board during his third year of service. The new chairman began to quote the mayor and city council to his fellow board members and to the superintendent, echoing his benefactors' belief that certain courses, including driver education, business arithmetic, and human relations, should be dropped from the curriculum and that the funds allocated for these courses should remain in the city budget rather than be transferred to the school budget. The issue received wide publicity, and factions began to form among the general public. One group was composed largely of businessmen who wanted to have the city council replace the entire school board. Another group, composed of unhappy parents, felt that false economy was being advocated and openly demanded that the city council stop interfering with the work of the school board. The members of the board became hostile toward its chairman. The chairman let it be known that, if the courses were not discontinued, he would talk to the members of the city council individually and request that the council cut the school budget approximately $75,000 for the next annual session. Finally, the controversial courses were discontinued at the request of the board, although the decision did not represent the true feeling of the board.

Case Number Two—Mr. Smith

This case took place in a county school system which was predominantly rural and whose major income was from agriculture. The school system had a 7-5 school organization; that is, 7 elementary grades and 5 high-school grades. Mr. Smith, the candidate for the board, was employed by the federal government and resided in the county. He was well educated, holding a Ph.D. degree from a leading university, and he was sold on the idea that the school board should change the school organization from a 7-5 plan to a 6-3-3 plan. He talked with many members of the community and extolled the virtues of having both a junior and a senior high school in each area where the existing high schools were located.

As he was a well-informed professional man, the candidate had a number of personal friends, and, after speaking to numerous PTA's, civic clubs, and other community groups, he was elected to the school board by popular vote.

The superintendent and the other members of the five-man board did not share the new board member's enthusiasm for the 6-3-3 plan of organization. Mr. Smith dominated the board meetings and frequently presented papers giving evidence favorable to his suggested organization. He had little respect for the administrator's views and even less for those of the other board members. Mr. Smith stated emphatically that the segment of the community which had elected him expected to see the present plan changed to a 6-3-3 organization. Other board members attempted to help Mr. Smith recognize that he had a responsibility as a board member to represent the entire school district, as did all the members, not just the geographic area where he resided. Although the new member succeeded for three years in keeping each meeting in a turmoil because of his continued insistence upon changing the school organization to conform with his campaign promises, the changes were not made.

What Is a Desirable Size for Local School Boards?

The size of school boards varies greatly. There are major differences among the states and also within many of them. In some states the size of the board is dependent upon state school laws. This is true in Louisiana, North Carolina, and Virginia. Perhaps the greatest variation between two states is in an Indiana township, where one member is permitted, and in Louisiana, where the number of police jurors in each district determines the number of board members and which may total nineteen. In 36 states all boards, except those where special legislation applies, fall within a range of three to seven members.

Large boards, which have nine or more members, are a subject of much controversy. Some of the problems faced by these boards are maintaining an interest in their work and in their individual responsibility, establishing standing committees to perform certain functions, becoming unwieldly and inept, and finding a common convenient time to hold regular and special meetings. Large boards provide more opportunities for the development of factions and cliques, since it is hard for all members to be present and to be heard on most problems.

Small boards of education, those having three or less members, have their troubles, too. With a small board it is very difficult to do an exhaustive and complete study on controversial questions. A board of three or fewer members is too small to present a variety of viewpoints or to make a variety of suggestions for action concerning the complicated problems school boards face.

The desirable size for a school board would seem to be one that is large enough to overcome the criticisms leveled at the extremely large and the unusually small boards. Authorities in the field of school administration recommend boards of five to seven members. A board of this size can avoid too much formality and is able to discuss realistically the problems of the school system. It is also advantageous to have an odd number of members. A motion may be lost in case of tie votes in even-numbered boards. It is even more difficult to pass a motion by a majority vote if the board is composed of an even number of members. Although large and small boards still may be found, the trend has been toward boards of five to seven members.

Of two cases presented to illustrate this issue, one exemplifies an unusually large board which resorts to the use of standing committees. The other case illustrates how a small board may become dependent on one member and may suffer from lack of ideas and stimulating discussions.

Case Number Three—Mrs. Green

A board of education, composed of twelve members elected by popular vote, had a great amount of trouble conducting the business of its school district. It became necessary for the members to do much of their business through the use of standing committees which reported to the full board for approval of their actions. Among the standing committees appointed were finance, school buildings and grounds, legislation, and complaints.

Although the exclusive functions of standing committees are difficult to define, the groups were told to hold separate meetings and then report to the entire board. All went well until the various committees began making recommendations to the entire board. Mrs. Green, a board member in her fifth year of service, and one who never took anything for granted, was serving as a member of the standing committee on finance. When the other committees began reporting, Mrs. Green insisted that the entire board consider both sides of every committee report under discussion.

Several members of the board felt that reports from standing committees should be adopted without discussion. Other members felt that this procedure would lead to the final decision being made by a rather small segment of the board. Still other members recognized Mrs. Green's point. Mrs. Green cited the impracticality of a committee considering problems which cut across more than one field. She gave as an example the fact that the finance committee was unable to make recommendations for school-plant repairs without meeting with the committee on school buildings. Mrs. Green further declared that it would be almost impossible for the actions of the board to be coordinated when four subboards were making the policies. After a long meeting a motion was made and passed to the effect that the board discontinue its standing committees and meet as a committee of the whole. This pleased the superintendent, as he felt that nonprofessional administration should not be substituted for professional administration.

Case Number Four—Mr. Adair

The board of education to which Mr. Adair belonged consisted of three members, all appointed by the governor. The county school system was a suburban district which had experienced rapid industrial growth and increased enrollments. Mr. Adair operated an independent grocery store near the center of the school district. He was in his mid-fifties. The other two board members, both men, were farmers, and each resided near the edge of the school district. Both of these board members had completed high school but never attended college. Mr. Adair had graduated from a small denominational college with a degree in business administration.

Board meetings were held in the school-board office in the community where Mr. Adair lived. Because of the heavy pressure of work, one of the other board members usually missed about half the meetings. Even when all three members were present, Mr. Adair made most of the suggestions. By nature, Mr. Adair was not the type of person to be dictatorial, but he seldom left a job half-completed. It was exceedingly difficult for Mr. Adair to get the other members of the board to disagree with him or to offer conflicting points of view. The two farmers were somewhat sensitive about their lack of formal training and generally left the opinions to Mr. Adair. In actual practice, Mr. Adair had a rubber-stamp board.

On one occasion a group of parents approached the board about the possibility of establishing kindergartens. The board agreed to study the problem with the superintendent and to report back to the parents. The two board members from the edge of the school district talked with a few people but came back to the next meeting with little to say. Mr. Adair did not wish to see the kindergarten program initiated; therefore, the superintendent was voted down, even though only one board member had really been opposed to the recommendation.

What Determines School-Board Effectiveness?

For many years it has been believed that certain traits were desirable in order for a school-board member to be effective. Among them were: the ability to spend the necessary time for study of school problems, an understanding of the local school system, willingness to defend board policy, a high degree of interest in public education, a desire to cooperate with the board and with the superintendent, and general characteristics of good citizenship. Of course, there is no magic formula for judging effective school-board members. It is unlikely that any single board member will possess all these traits.

In addition to the traits which authorities specifically recommend, an effective school-board member should possess the attitude of a learner; he should have a desire to improve his knowledge of the practices and problems of the school system within which he works; and he should understand that his function is not to run the school system but to see that the superintendent and other school employees operate the district satisfactorily.

Barnhart [2] has shed new light on this subject by securing from superintendents and school-board members, through the

[2] Richard E. Barnhart, *The Critical Requirements for School Board Members Based Upon an Analysis of Critical Incidents,* unpublished doctor's dissertation, Indiana University, Bloomington, 1952.

critical-incident technique, written descriptions of incidents considered critical in determining effective and ineffective behavior in school-board action. His samples came from communities of over 2,500 population and were scattered over 12 states. He secured 741 critical incidents which gave examples of effective and ineffective behavior. He found that ineffective-behavior incidents were greatest in the area of board unity. The critical requirements within this area included subordinating self-interests, adhering to the policy-making functions of the board, accepting and supporting majority decisions, identifying self with board policies and actions, and refusing to speak or act independently of the board.

The largest number of effective-behavior incidents fell in the area of leadership. These resulted from ability to suspend judgment until the facts were gathered, ability to make use of experience, ability to identify problems, ability to see workable solutions, willingness to devote time to board work outside of meetings, acceptance of ideas of others, and a deep interest in the schools.

The results of several studies concerning school boards were coordinated and reported by Stapley [3] through the Midwest Administrative Center of the Cooperative Project in Educational Administration. These studies reveal that effectiveness increases with school-board experience through the first six years. The amount of formal education of a member, his economic success, and the amount of time he can devote to public education are closely related to successful board membership. The more successful boards tend to be those that adhere to

[3] Maurice E. Stapley, "School Board Studies," *Studies in Educational Administration,* Midwest Administration Center, University of Chicago, Chicago, 1957.

written policies and encourage their members to take part in meetings of school-board associations.

Case Number Five depicts the ineffective behavior of a board member who refuses to accept and support the majority decision of the board. Case Number Six exemplifies the effective behavior of a board member who demonstrates his ability to identify a problem and to see a workable solution.

Case Number Five—Mr. Wade

The scene of this school-board example was in a small city school district. The board was composed of five members elected by popular vote. The school district had experienced rapid growth in pupil enrollment since World War II. One member, Mr. Wade, was a strongly opinionated person. For example, when the board voted four to one to discontinue its policy of permitting outside groups to use the school gymnasium for public dancing, Mr. Wade protested vigorously and became very upset. He voted against changing the policy and lectured the other members about their lack of understanding of community problems. Mr. Wade went about his daily work but consistently told newspaper reporters, the local radio-station director, and others that he did not vote for changing the policy on use of the school gymnasium, and, therefore, he felt no obligation to defend the action of the board. Some of the other board members thought that Mr. Wade acted as he did because he did not want to upset any community group or person, since he operated a local five-and-ten-cent store within the community.

The next time Mr. Wade stood for election he was defeated by a large vote. The other board members remained firm in their policy, and their problem was partially resolved.

Case Number Six—Mr. Seymour

The chairman of a local board of education received an anonymous letter accusing the cafeteria manager of the comprehensive high school of serving larger portions of food to some pupils than to others. The board took up the matter for discussion and action at its monthly meeting which followed within a few days. The superintendent and board members read the letter rather carefully. Two of the board members suggested that the letter agreed with rumors they had previously heard about the cafeteria manager, and they immediately proposed that she be dismissed. The superintendent and Mr. Seymour, chairman of the board, disagreed with this idea. They suggested that such hasty action was not desirable. Mr. Seymour pointed out that the cafeteria manager had been with the school for five years and that he had heard only praise for her work. Furthermore, Mr. Seymour recommended that the letter be burned and that no mention be made of it in the board minutes. It was his feeling that anyone who had a serious and justifiable complaint against school personnel should appear before the board with written charges and should discuss them.

The board agreed to destroy the letter and asked the superintendent to discuss its contents with the cafeteria manager. It also recommended that more recognition be given to the significance of lunchrooms in all the schools, and that every effort be extended to inform parents and others about their operation.

How Does One Distinguish Between the Functions of the School Board and Those of the Superintendent?

Most state laws give practically all powers and duties pertaining to the management of the schools to the board and give few, if any, to the superintendent. Since so many of his powers are secured from the school board, the best-qualified superintendent cannot be very successful without its cooperation and support. Recent studies have evidenced the fact that lack of understanding of the responsibilities and limits of their jobs is a major source of board-administrator trouble.

As the chief executive officer of the local school board, the superintendent occupies a position somewhat comparable to that of a general manager of a large industrial plant or the executive head of an important business enterprise, with additional responsibilities not found in either business or industry. The school board is his board of directors.

As the person trained in the technical aspects of administration, the superintendent must carry out the all-important advisory function. He should be very careful to present only those recommendations which he has considered thoroughly and is convinced are sound. His advice should stem from his recognition of the needs of the school district and be based upon his wide training and experience. He must be patient with board members who do not see problems in the same light. It is necessary for the superintendent to practice acceptable professional and business methods in order to have good working relationships with the board.

It was once thought that the board had the function of employing the superintendent but that, once he was employed, professional matters were mainly in his hands. In several states there is no requirement that a superintendent be employed, but it is within the board's discretionary power, and the need for a superintendent is usually recognized. It is possible, however, for a superintendent who is elected by popular vote to feel responsible to the people (irrespective of the provisions of the law) rather than to the board.

Although the compilation of written policies for a school

board is no cure-all, it has been found that boards which have a clear-cut statement of basic policies tend to be more effective. The writing of school-board policies should not be done in a hurried manner; it should be developed as a learning experience for board members and administrators.

The real crux of this issue lies in the fact that administrators and board members do not agree on where policy making stops and administration begins. Sletten [4] analyzed the opinions of board members and superintendents on several matters of policy. In one phase of his study, superintendents and board members were asked to react to the following statement: "The administrator should generally try to save face for staff members and to support them in their decisions even though on particular occasions their judgments are in error." Of those who agreed with this statement, 79 per cent were superintendents and only 41 per cent were board members.

Pritchard,[5] in a study of 60 small districts in Nebraska and Iowa, where opinions of board members, superintendents, and teachers were secured through the use of an interviewer's guide, found that activities which appear to provide the greatest harmony are those in which the board and superintendent work together in the development of policy. Dissatisfaction with the procedure in use is more likely in those areas in which either the board or the superintendent exercises major authority without mutual consultation.

It is rather clear, from this brief analysis of the relationship between the board and the superintendent, that the control of

---

[4] Vernon O. Sletten, *A Related Study of the Opinions of Montana School Board Members and Superintendents on Selected Board Policy Practices,* unpublished doctor's dissertation, University of Oregon, Eugene, 1954.

[5] George S. Pritchard, *Duties and Responsibilities of School Board Members in Small District Schools,* unpublished doctor's dissertation, Michigan State College, East Lansing, 1953.

the schools is not the business of either party acting alone but is, in many instances, a cooperative endeavor. Both groups must work together harmoniously for the good of the pupils and the community they represent. The minor division of duties—legislative and judicial for the board and administrative for the superintendent—is not made to relieve anyone of duties or to deprive anyone of authority or recognition; it is meant to provide an efficient organization to help increase the possibilities of a better education for the youth of our land.

The example of board behavior given in Case Number Seven illustrates what can happen when the board takes over the superintendent's function of nominating and recommending the personnel to be employed. Case Number Eight is an example of the board and the superintendent working together to solve a problem relating to school policy at the attendance unit level.

Case Number Seven—Mrs. Popper

It was a policy in the Centerville district for the superintendent to recommend both professional and nonprofessional employees to the local board for appointment. An elderly lady who had taught in the adjoining district for a number of years and was related to Mrs. Popper, a board member, sought employment as an elementary teacher in Centerville. Although she was well aware of the local policy, the applicant did not apply to the superintendent. Instead, she talked with Mrs. Popper, who told the applicant she could consider herself employed.

At the regular monthly meeting of the board, Mrs. Popper brought up the applicant's name and qualifications. The superintendent was surprised and questioned the irregular procedure. He was informed by Mrs. Popper that this distant relative of hers had already been promised a position, for the following year, by herself and two of the remaining board members. The applicant was appointed by a three-to-two vote of the board and without the recommendation of the superintendent. The appointee taught two years and retired because of poor health. The superintendent moved to a better position one year later.

Case Number Eight—Mr. Watson

Mr. Watson, a member of the board of education in the Pleasantville school district, received a series of telephone calls from parents one Friday evening, suggesting that he, as chairman of the board, have the head football coach dismissed because the coach had moved five of the first-team members to the second team. The coach had previously given the boys fair notice that if they broke training rules, which included getting to bed by 10 P.M. each evening unless engaged in a school activity, they would be punished. No other members of the football team or their parents had complained. The five boys in question had acknowledged staying out for two consecutive evenings until after midnight. Their parents felt that the coach had gone too far.

Mr. Watson asked the parents to take the matter up with the coach and the high-school principal, since this was a problem that pertained only to one school. The complainants were told to contact the superintendent and ask him to place the problem on the agenda for the next board meeting and to appear in person before the board, along with the principal and coach, if they were unable to resolve the problem. The board member advised the superintendent of his actions. Since the board and the superintendent heard nothing further about this problem, it can be assumed that it was worked out in a satisfactory manner.

Should the School Board Evaluate
the Educational Program?

One of the most complex duties of the local board is that of appraisal, yet appraisal and approval are among the most common functions of school boards. The superintendent recommends patterns of action, and it becomes the duty of the board to evaluate each recommendation and proposal. It is also essential that the board continually appraise the program and all phases that contribute to its success or failure.

On many occasions board members have been asked to make decisions without adequate information upon which to base such decisions. Boards must constantly react to many conflicting pressures, especially with regard to the school program. The classroom is the heart of the school system and should be of primary interest to the board as well as to the professional staff. With the recommendation of the superintendent, it becomes the responsibility of the board to decide what improvements should be attempted, the order in which they should be undertaken, and the manner of payment for the needed services.

Board members are not experts in education, but they can become acquainted with the schools and their problems. School-board members can obtain a general understanding of public education by visiting schools; reading books, periodicals, and other materials prepared for school-board members; attending meetings of state and national school-board associations; having selected members of the faculty appear before the board each month and explain some phase of the school program; and asking the superintendent questions about the program. An alert superintendent can help provide school-board meetings with programs which stimulate and help board members to become better informed. It might be good for some boards to begin with a self-evaluation. This would afford the members an opportunity to review the way in which the board handles its policy-making and other responsibilities. But, regardless of the training a board member receives, he must continue to recognize that he is not an expert in professional matters pertaining to education. The board should constantly seek the advice and counsel of the superintendent and other professional persons suggested by him.

With essential information and advice about the program, and with an open mind, the board is fully capable of reaching decisions about evaluation of the school program. It is doubtful if any proposal which cannot be expressed in terms readily understandable by the intelligent laymen who compose the school boards and cannot be supported by reasoning which appeals to their sound judgment has a place in any system of public education.

Case Number Nine cites an illustration of a school board attempting to carry out an evaluation of the school program. It also indicates that school-board members should not interfere with the technical aspects of teaching and grading. In Case Number Ten the school board and the superintendent sought and found help from the professional staff in evaluating the teaching of reading.

Case Number Nine—Mrs. Johnson

Immediately after the Russians orbited their first satellite, two leading newspapers sent their representatives out to interview people on the street about public education. The reporters wanted to know, "Are American public schools tough enough on the pupils?" Although this sample of public opinion was very limited in scope and not truly representative (there was no random sample of the population taken), the newspapers began to run stories based on the answers their reporters had received about how easy our present-day schools are. A member of the local board, Mrs. Johnson, who held a degree from a liberal arts women's college, and who believed that public schools should operate to educate only the top 15 per cent of our youth, began to collect the newspaper items which made it appear that all public schools had neglected to fail a large number of poor students. She called many leading citizens in the community, telling them that the newspapers were telling the true story of the local schools. Some of the citizens did not take time to gather facts; they called the superintendent and board chairman and demanded that the grading system be changed from Excellent, Satisfactory, and Unsatisfactory to percentage grades. They felt that this would make it more difficult for teachers to pass unprepared students to a higher class.

At the next meeting of the board, Mrs. Johnson brought up the idea that the board should inaugurate a policy changing the grading system from E, S, and U to letter grades based on percentages. A heated discussion followed, in which the superintendent advised against such action and recommended that the professional staff be permitted to study the grading system and make a report to the board before changing the policy. By a three-to-two vote, Mrs. Johnson was able to get the policy change through the board without the recommendation of the superintendent.

The new policy was put into effect the next fall. The school board received more telephone calls concerning this policy change than about any other it had made in recent years. The teachers in the system felt that the board had dictated the change of a policy involving technical aspects of instruction about which it was ill informed. Administrators within the system found it difficult to support a policy which they had no part in making and did not believe workable. The next steps are uncertain; although Mrs. Johnson won her point, there is strong feeling within the community that the problem has not been solved.

Case Number Ten—Mr. Barron

The local school board of a large city had jurisdiction over an elementary-school district. There were twelve or thirteen elementary districts within the metropolitan area, and one high-school district superimposed over the elementary districts. Each district had a local board of education and a superintendent. The particular district in question had more than its share of elementary pupils and was not blessed with abundant financial support. A large percentage of the pupils were Spanish Americans.

A number of parents called Mr. Barron, chairman of the board, and reported that their children were not being taught to read properly. Other parents visited Mr. Barron and complained that the phonic method was not being used in the teaching of reading. Mr. Barron reported the complaints to the board and the superintendent. After much debate, the board decided it knew little or nothing about the reading program. The chairman asked the superintendent if it would be possible to have school personnel present to the board some information relative to the teaching of reading. The superintendent thought the suggestion was excellent and followed through by having a special board meeting in which the elementary supervisor and selected teachers explained to the board and superintendent how reading was being taught. The board members were happy to learn that the school system had an excellent reading program in operation. Phonics was utilized not as an end in itself but as a tool which children could use. Members of the board expressed appreciation for this helpful experience. Although the board members realized that they were not experts in the field of reading, they did feel that this background information helped them to defend the program to the public and to support the work of the faculty which they had appointed.

Should Boards of Education Spend School Funds to Join State and National School-Board Associations?

Perhaps the best test of this issue is whether the purposes served by state and national school-board associations are of enough value to justify the cost to the local board which joins its state association. If so, it is only fair that fees be paid from school-district funds.

Some boards feel that the money which goes for dues should be spent to take care of pressing financial problems; some are not in sympathy with the policies of the state and national associations; others feel that the money which would be paid out in dues should be spent to buy consultant help and services which are better fitted to local needs than those provided by state and national associations; and a few boards are discouraged from joining by their superintendents, for fear that the board will want to take over the technical aspects of administration.

It is doubtful if any of these arguments against joining state and national associations is really defensible. Rather than attempt to refute each argument individually, it is better to consider the work of state and national school-board associations and to examine the questions in the light of services offered.

The primary purpose of state-board development, since its inception in Pennsylvania more than sixty years ago, has been to provide services to local boards of education, to serve as an agency for strengthening and upgrading school-board service. (In most states, courts have decided that dues to state associations are legal expenditures of school districts, although in some states special legislation has been necessary to secure this right. Most state associations base their dues on the size of the district, the assessed valuation of the school district, or the size of the local operational budget, but a number of other criteria may also be used.) Providing orientation for new board members and advancing the in-service growth of experienced board members are two of the more important ways in which school-board associations can give leadership to local boards.[6] More specific services which state school-board associations may provide include better school legislation, larger school districts, better salaries and welfare provisions for teachers, increased state support, better public-school business administraton, and improved state school-building codes.

Every school superintendent should strongly recommend that his board join its state and national associations. He should likewise encourage active participation on the part of the board members in these organizations. Generally, superintendents are associate members and have all the rights and privileges of active members except those of voting and holding office.

The National School Boards Association works at the national level to help all fifty state associations reach their mutual goals. The National Association performs services and undertakes informational activities and research for which the individual state associations are not equipped. It is dedicated to

[6] Stapley, *op. cit.,* p. 50.

helping the public understand the significance of school-board service to American public education and to the democratic way of life. Research has indicated that board members are more effective when they participate in state and national organization, when they share ideas with others, and when they have opportunities to work and learn about public schools.

Case Number Eleven illustrates how boards of education may build upon false premises in their arguments for not joining state and national associations. In Case Number Twelve we see how one board member, who really understood and appreciated the work of his state and national organizations, was able to convince the board and superintendent of the value of membership.

Case Number Eleven—Mr. Kay

The local board of education in a rather wealthy community found that its dues to join its state association would be almost $500 for the year. The school district could easily make such an expenditure, but the board's new chairman, Mr. Kay, felt that money previously paid to the state association had not produced tangible results. The other four board members and the superintendent did not see why the board should not affiliate with the state association as it had in the past. As Mr. Kay talked, two of the board members began to share his doubt. Mr. Kay, an accountant by profession, still thought that the state association could not contribute as much to the in-service training of the local board as could two or three national speakers who could be brought in to discuss selected phases of school-board work. The board put off its decision on joining the state association until its next monthly meeting.

At its next meeting, Mr. Kay again persuaded the board

to delay joining for another month. The two board members who favored joining did get Mr. Kay to agree to invite a representative from the state association to discuss the increased dues and services with the local board, but even after hearing the representative from the state association, the board voted not to affiliate with the state association until the following year. This delay, the board decided, would give the members a chance to evaluate the increased services of the association.

The following year the board did join the association, and Mr. Kay was appointed to the executive committee of the state association. He made several helpful suggestions to the executive committee, including ways of improving the accounting system of the association, and has since become a leader in state and national school-board associations.

Case Number Twelve—Mrs. Scott

This local board of education had responsibility for a county school district in an area which had many pupils and little wealth. Mrs. Scott had been on the board for over twenty years. Her formal education was limited to high school, but she had learned much during her twenty-odd years on the school board. Mrs. Scott had served as chairman of the board for several years and had held offices in the state and national associations. She was a productive leader of her own board and a valuable association worker.

One year the state association voted to increase its services to the local board and, for the first time, to pay full dues to the national association. This made it necessary to increase the local board's dues to the state association. Two or three members of Mrs. Scott's board began to question the advisability of paying out almost $400 to join the state association, although they did appreciate its work. Mrs. Scott called a special board meeting in which she asked each member to list the services the board had received from the association. Also, Mrs. Scott gave an overview of what the state association planned for the next two years. After weighing the evidence, the board unanimously voted to join again. The superintendent complimented the board for its sincere study of the problem and expressed his pleasure about its decision.

Questions for Discussion

Case Number One

1. Assume that you are superintendent of schools. What would you do? What would you say to Mr. Brown? What would be your next steps in dealing with the school board?

2. As a member of this school board, what kind of help can you give to the superintendent? Should you support the board decision or attempt to convince other members that the board has made a decision that will be hard to support?

Case Number Two

3. Who should decide the plan of organization for a school district? Is this the job of the school board, of the superintendent, of the faculty, or of the community?

4. Assume that you were superintendent. What action could you have taken to help Mr. Smith understand his behavior as a school-board member? Do you believe Mr. Smith would have acted differently if he had been an appointed board member?

Case Number Three

5. What dangers are involved in having several standing committees on school boards? What advantages?

6. When does a school board become too large to function effectively? Assume that you are chairman of a large school board. What suggestions can you make for efficient and smooth operation of such a board?

Case Number Four

7. When does a school board become too small to function effectively? What are the advantages and disadvantages of small school boards?

8. If you were superintendent in this case, what would you do to stimulate more discussion on problems of a controversial nature? How would you explain the board's action to the community?

Case Number Five

9. Is a board member ever justified in refusing to accept and to support the majority decision of the board? Was Mr. Wade justified in his actions?

10. As superintendent of this school district, what would you have done to help Mr. Wade understand his role as a board member? Does the chairman of the board of education have a responsibility to help other board members understand their roles? Why?

Case Number Six

11. What action would you have taken had you been the chairman of the board? Should anonymous letters be discussed at length during school-board meetings? Why?

12. How would you appraise the action of the superintendent in this case? Did he give adequate support to his staff?

Case Number Seven

13. What do you think of Mrs. Popper's behavior as a board member? Had you been chairman of the board, what action would you have taken?

14. What principles of administration were violated? How could the superintendent explain to other faculty members, and to the community, the action of the board?

Case Number Eight

15. Do you agree with Mr. Watson's way of handling this case? Why?

16. If you had been the superintendent in this case, would you have followed the advice of the board chairman? Why?

Case Number Nine

17. Was the action of Mrs. Johnson in accordance with the behavior of an effective board member trying to evaluate the school program? Why?

18. Should board members get involved in the technical aspects of instruction?

Case Number Ten

19. What do you think of Mr. Barron's behavior as a school-board member?

20. How could the problem have been handled differently?

Case Number Eleven

21. Why did Mr. Kay object to his board joining the state school-board association? Was he justified? Why?

22. How far should a board go in orienting its own members before taking action that might split the board?

Case Number Twelve

23. What do you have to say in regard to Mrs. Scott's behavior as a board member?

24. Do you agree with the superintendent's role in this case? Why?

Selected Readings

American Association of School Administrators, *School Boards in Action,* Twenty-fourth Yearbook, The Association, Washington, D.C., 1946; *School Board—Superintendent Relationships,* The Association, Washington, D.C., 1956; *Written Policies for School Boards,* The Association, Washington, D.C., 1955.

Barnhart, Richard E., *The Critical Requirements for School Board Members Based Upon an Analysis of Critical Incidents,* unpublished doctor's dissertation, Indiana University, Bloomington, 1952.

Guba, Egon, and Bidwell, Charles E., "Administrative Relationships," *Studies in Educational Administration,* Midwest Administration Center, University of Chicago, Chicago, 1957.

Hall, Morrill M., *Provisions for Local Boards of Education,* Bulletin No. 13, Office of Education, U.S. Department of Health, Education, and Welfare, Washington, D.C., 1957.

Jones, James J., "Some Activities and Responsibilities of School Boards in Public Relations," *Educational Administration and Supervision,* 39: 414–421, November, 1953.

Moore, Hollis A., Jr., *Studies in School Administration,* The American Association of School Administrators, Washington, D.C., 1957.

Pritchard, George S., *Duties and Responsibilities of School Board Members in Small District Schools,* unpublished doctor's dissertation, Michigan State College, East Lansing, 1953.

Reeder, Ward G., *School Boards and Superintendents,* The Macmillan Company, New York, 1954.

Reeves, Charles E., *School Boards: Their Status, Functions, and Activities,* Prentice-Hall, Inc., Englewood Cliffs, N.J., 1954.

Sampson, Gordon E., *School Board Effectiveness and the Tenure of the Administrator,* unpublished doctor's dissertation, University of Chicago, Chicago, 1955.

Sletten, Vernon O., *A Related Study of the Opinions of Montana School Board Members and Superintendents on Selected Board Practices,* unpublished doctor's dissertation, University of Oregon, Eugene, 1954.

Stapley, Maurice E., "School Board Studies," *Studies in Educational Administration,* Midwest Administration Center, University of Chicago, Chicago, 1957.

ISSUES DEALING WITH FINANCE, BUDGET PREPARATION, AND CONTROL

3.

ONE very complex and controversial problem involved in school public relations has to do with preparation of the budget, its controls, and the financing of the entire public-school system. There have been numerous unwarranted criticisms of school costs, many of which come from persons who have little knowledge about school expenditures and have no way of knowing if too much money is being spent for certain aspects of the program.

A major factor of any educational program is the level of financial support provided. Areas that are rich in tax resources can usually support an excellent program, but the poorer districts must make great sacrifices to support even a limited program. In many instances, factors relating to the size of a district operate against adequate financing; in others, no matter what the size, the tax base is so narrow that an adequate educational program cannot be supported even with a high tax rate.

Matters such as fiscal independence, local sources of revenue, federal aid to education, the spending of public funds for nonpublic schools, and the spending of public funds for school public relations are issues which need more study if our public-relations programs are to be effective. Today, as never before, the public school must compete for each dollar it receives for educating the youth of our land.

Should School Districts Be Fiscally Independent?

A majority of the school districts in the United States are independent of the other units of local government. In cities or counties which operate under charters or special acts of the legislature, there are almost as many variations of municipal or county control as there are cities or counties thus governed. These controls are exercised by various municipal or county bodies, either through direct acts or through determination of tax rates. Many states have enacted laws which establish minimums below which the school tax rate may not go and maximums which boards of education cannot exceed without a vote of the people of the school district. In some cities, and in some states, the financing of the schools of the local districts is under almost complete control of the local government rather than of the school boards.

A school system in which the board of education has the legal right to levy taxes and to spend the income thus gathered without securing the approval of some governmental agency, such as the mayor or city council, is said to have fiscal independence. If the board of education must have its budget approved by the local government and/or if the tax rate is set by the governing body, that school system is said to be fiscally dependent. In a majority of the states, boards of education are fiscally independent, and the tendency during recent years has been for that majority to increase. Of course, there are various degrees and types of fiscal independence or fiscal dependence.

Generally, authorities in school administration strongly favor fiscal independence, whereas, on the contrary, authorities in political science ordinarily urge a system whereby the public schools depend upon local government for financial support. The arguments for and against fiscally independent school districts have been summarized by a number of authorities. Among the most significant are those of Holmstedt, Burke, and the National Education Association.[1]

Arguments favoring fiscal independence include:

1. Education is a state function, and there should be no intermediary authority between the school board and the state.

2. School boards should be relatively free from political controls.

3. Fiscal control is ultimately connected with the selection of personnel.

4. Fiscally independent boards of education have not been extravagant.

5. The general fiscal authority, in determining the school budget, assumes responsibility for school policies.

6. The fiscally dependent board of education must waste time and energy presenting its budget to another authority.

7. Fiscal independence is the only way to protect school funds from being diverted to nonschool purposes.

8. Authority to determine school tax levies should be vested in the body responsible for the school program.

9. The cost of schools administered under the dependent and independent organizations are about equal.

10. Continuity in the development and maintenance of the

[1] Raleigh W. Holmstedt, "Fiscal Controls," *Problems and Issues in Public School Finance,* The National Conference of Professors of Educational Administration, Teachers College, Columbia University, New York, 1952, Chap. IX; Arvid J. Burke, *Financing Public Schools in the United States,* Harper & Brothers, New York, 1957, Chap. VII; and National Education Association, "Fiscal Authority of City School Boards," *Research Bulletin,* **24:** 47–78, April, 1950.

educational program is more certainly guaranteed where the board of education has full control.

11. There are very few advantages in combining school financing accounting and municipal accounting, since they are no different.

Arguments favoring fiscal dependence include:

1. Municipal officials are forced to assume responsibility for tax levies over which they have little or no control.

2. Determining expenditures for all purposes should allow one demand to be weighed against another.

3. Education is a state responsibility only to the extent that the state helps finance it.

4. Coordination of services in which the schools and municipality are mutually interested is facilitated.

5. There is need for a unified and coordinated local financial structure.

6. Fiscal independence brings no positive assurance of freedom from politics.

Much research has been conducted on this issue, but the facts which have been collected by political scientists and school administrators do not provide conclusive favorable evidence for either point of view; from the standpoint of educational policy and effect on educational programs, however, the evidence tends to favor fiscal independence.

The first case illustrates how the board of education of a fiscally dependent school district may waste time and energy presenting its budget to another authority, and how the district itself may have needed school funds spent for nonschool purposes.

The second case depicts a fiscally independent school district which has political difficulties that weaken its school program.

Case Number One—Cedartown

Cedartown is a local school district which is dependent upon the city council for its budget. A problem developed over part of the school district's budget being diverted to nonschool purposes. Two years previously, the superintendent and board had recommended that kindergartens be organized for the school district. This recommendation was based upon more than a year's intensive study, by the board and by selected citizens, of the need for kindergartens. Members of the community group had expressed a willingness to support higher taxes in order to have them.

During the summer the city council refused to accept the school budget as long as it contained a request for funds to operate kindergarten programs. The board of education and the superintendent requested and got a joint meeting with the city council. Again, the budget was not approved, since it contained a request for funds to finance this program. Finally, the school board had to obey the city council and remove from the budget the request for funds to finance kindergarten programs in order to get its budget approved.

The money which would have gone, under ordinary circumstances, to support the kindergarten program, went instead to build sidewalks within the city. Three of the board members resigned, and they were immediately replaced by three new appointees who thought less of kindergarten programs. The following year the superintendent moved to a larger and better school district. Many citizens of the school district lost faith in the school board and the city council.

Case Number Two—Blackberry Hill

The school district of Blackberry Hill encompasses a small village of 500 people and the surrounding area. The total pupil enrollment is approximately 3,500. The five-member board of education is elected by popular vote, as is the superintendent. The school district is fiscally independent.

Since the surrounding area is largely agricultural, all of the three high schools offered vocational agriculture and home economics as part of their curriculums. One teacher of vocational agriculture conducted adult classes monthly in each of the four large communities of the county and cultivated quite a group of new friends, most of whom were interested in making the high-school curriculums contain more vocational and fewer college-preparation courses. After teaching adult classes for two semesters in each of the four community centers of the county, the teacher informed the superintendent that he intended to run for the superintendency. He campaigned vigorously and won the election by a wide margin. In keeping with his promises, he got the board to reduce the English requirement for graduation to three years and the mathematics to one year. More vocational subjects were added. The board offered little resistance; several of its members had voted for the new superintendent. Later, three of these board members requested that the superintendent buy school supplies and fuel from them. The suggestion was resisted by the superintendent, and the resulting ill feeling continued until the superintendent was defeated for re-election along with two of the three board members.

What Local Sources of Revenue Should Be Used to Support Public Education?

Although the property tax has often been criticized, it remains the major source of public-school revenues on the local level. This tax usually includes general, real, and classified property taxes. The property tax accounts for more than half of the financial support for school revenue, and, as a producer of revenue, it cannot be replaced easily. The property tax provides a leeway for the local school district to obtain local revenue over and above state and federal support. This freedom permits local school districts to obtain the necessary funds for experimentation and research. Even though the property tax has many weaknesses, it is likely to remain a major source of school revenue.

One criterion of a sound tax is that it can be administered fairly and efficiently. One of the difficulties encountered with the property tax is discrepancy between assessment and true value. Poor assessment practices result in large losses of revenue to local communities. The more nearly one reaches 100 per cent appraisal, the more equitable is the property tax. If property is assessed as a small per cent of its true value, the tax tends to become regressive in that it taxes the small property owner out of proportion.

Another difficulty with the property tax is the number of exemptions that have been permitted to creep in over a period of time. Among these are state properties; properties of educational, religious, and charitable organizations; and some business properties. Former servicemen or their widows and dependents may have limited property-tax exemptions, and a number of states exempt local property tax through homestead exemption, up to the first $5,000 of assessed valuation.

Responsibility for the collection of school taxes varies in different states, but it is generally the county treasurer or municipal collector who actually makes the collection. Irrespective of who is charged with the responsibility of assessing, levying, and collecting school taxes, accurate records should be kept and exemption and assessment policies should be made public.

The declining significance of property taxes in local support for schools has been due partially to exemptions and restrictions established during depression years. Any sound revenue program for public schools has a place for a tax that is stable and yields large amounts of revenue. Exemptions and assessments need continuous study and appraisal.

Nonproperty taxes and other sources that have contributed to local school revenue include poll taxes, income from parking meters, fines and forfeitures, permanent school funds, tuition, sales taxes, income taxes, and taxes on admissions and amusements, tobacco, utilities, gambling devices, soft drinks, and motor vehicles. Many of these sources of income can be used only by large cities, whereas others are not desirable forms of taxation because they hit hardest those who are least able to pay. In addition, the income from such taxes fluctuates with the business cycle.

Although the property tax may not continue to be the one major source of school revenue, it should be maintained, and its assessment practices and methods of collection should be improved. Meanwhile, additional research should be conducted to seek other local sources of revenues to supplement the property tax.

The example given in Case Number Three illustrates what can happen when the local property tax is the major source of revenue and excessive exemptions are permitted on property.

The illustration presented in Case Number Four exemplifies how a local school district sought and found other sources of revenue to supplement the property tax for school support.

Case Number Three—Beaconville

This small town is located in a fast-growing area of 2,100 residents. Its main source of income is from winter tourists and small businesses.

Although there had been much recent construction of homes in the school district, the property-tax revenue had not been excessive. Most of the homes are not worth more than $10,000 to $12,000 in true value. The state passed a homestead exemption law which exempted all homes from tax on the first $5,000 of assessed valuation. Thus many property owners had their individual property taxes for the year reduced from about $200 per year to approximately $25. In some extreme cases, individuals paid less than $12 for the year.

The total revenue now available from the local property taxes was less than one third of what it had been for the previous year. Much of the local fund had previously been spent to lift the salaries of teachers above the state's minimum salary schedule. Upon loss of this revenue, more than a third of the seventy-odd teachers employed by the district resigned and accepted better-paying teaching positions elsewhere. The total school program was, of course, weakened. Since most laymen knew little about the tax equity and were adverse to property taxes, the community did practically nothing to replace the lost revenue. Now, after two years, Beaconville school district is being reluctantly forced to consider a higher tax rate on assessed valuation of local property.

Case Number Four—Smokeyville

The town of Smokeyville is located in a remote mountainous area. It is a progressive town of some 12,000 inhabitants. The schools within the town have always been accepted by the local community as being somewhat above the average for the state. The principal source of local revenue for many years had been the property tax. The state legislature passed a homestead exemption act which excluded the first $3,500 of assessed home valuation from being taxed. Immediately, the local school board, the superintendent, and the tax assessment board held a joint meeting. This group agreed to raise the tax rate on the assessed valuation of property for the following year. In addition, citizen groups were organized by the combined group to encourage legislation which would permit the town of Smokeyville to levy a ½ per cent local sales tax. This ½ per cent was to be added to the already existing 2½ per cent state sales tax. The next legislature passed special measures which enabled Smokeyville to levy a ½ per cent local sales tax. The school district is in good financial condition, and its citizens appear to resent the local sales tax less than the property tax, even though very few items are exempt from the sales tax.

To What Extent Should the Federal Government Aid Public Education?

It has been assumed by state and federal courts that education is a state function. The public schools and the public institutions of higher education operate under state law and receive their support through provisions made by the several states and their political subdivisions. But, though the Constitution of the United States makes no direct mention of education, the federal government has actually developed extensive relations with education. In addition to engaging in educational undertakings of its own, the federal government cooperates with states and their subdivisions and with public and private educational institutions in the conduct of numerous educational enterprises. It is no longer a question of "Will there be federal aid to education?" but rather "To what extent should the federal government aid education?"

Through land grants, money grants, emergency and relief measures, national defense and war, the education of veterans, and a host of other federal activities in education, the federal government does provide aid to education. The early land and monetary grants for education involved practically no federal control of the education so aided beyond specifying the types of institutions as beneficiaries. A new principle was written into educational law with the passage of the Marine School Act in 1911, under which a state or municipality was to receive from federal appropriations for such schools a sum of money not to exceed the amount appropriated by the state or municipality. A matching requirement, in some form or other, has since that time found a place in other federal-aid legislation for education.

Since 1918, efforts have been made in practically every Congress to obtain federal aid for elementary and secondary education, but powerful opponents have succeeded in preventing enactment of such legislation. Support for this type of legislation, however, has been widespread. Most of the bills that have been introduced have recognized state control of education and, in general, they have contained provisions for federal control only to the extent necessary to assure that the federal funds are expended for the purposes stated in the law.

The need for federal aid to education has been pointed out by many authorities in school finance. Among the more cogent reasons for such aid are inequality in educational opportunities among the various states, migrations which bring into a community products of school systems at variance with its own, financial inequalities among various states, variation in number of children to be educated among the states, promotion of national defense, and upgrading the competency of federal employees.

It is doubtful if equal educational opportunities can be provided in the United States without federal support. Only by taxing the wealth where it exists and distributing it to areas where it does not can the entire United States hope to achieve equal educational opportunities.

There are many Americans, however, who do not believe in federal support for education. Most of their arguments are well known: Federal aid eventually means federal control; education is a state function, not a federal one; if the federal government will return some of its taxing power to the states, they will be able to educate without federal assistance; and some states will pay more in taxes than they will receive in aid. Some Americans believe in federal aid but feel it should go to the weak states, not the strong; and some feel that federal aid should go to nonpublic as well as to public schools.

Many of the arguments commonly made in opposition to federal aid to education are more closely related to fears of what might happen than they are to actual facts. Federal aid to education has been in operation, in some form or other, since the First Morrill Act of 1862, which provided funds for military training and for education in agriculture and the mechanic arts. It is extremely doubtful if public education can take care of its increased enrollment without increased federal and state aid.

The example given in Case Number Five illustrates some of

the controls that are attached to federal aid to vocational education and also the reaction of a community to the controls.

The sixth case illustrates the role of the federal government in supporting public schools in an area where they would not otherwise be possible.

Case Number Five—Maple Valley

The school district that includes Maple Valley is a county school system serving a rather sparsely populated area, with Maple Valley, a town of 5,000 inhabitants, the approximate geographic and population center. There are three other high schools in the county. Most of the people in this community are farmers, or their work in some way involves providing goods and services to farmers.

Each high school has a program of vocational education. For many years this was a cooperative program, with federal aid provided on a matching basis. But other high-school teachers began to object to the teachers of vocational agriculture not being assigned home-room duties, bus duty, hall duty, or other such school tasks. To be eligible for federal support, the system could not permit the teachers of vocational education to teach outside their field or to teach large classes. Since the four high schools were small and the population sparse, teachers of other subjects sometimes had to teach classes of forty to fifty pupils.

After several complaints, the teachers got together and suggested to the superintendent, and he to the board of education, that vocational agriculture continue to be offered in the school system, but that it be offered without qualifying for federal support. The board made the change in policy, and the school district of Maple Valley today does not have Smith-Hughes aid for vocational agriculture. Of course, this means that the local district must collect more revenue in order to bear the burden of cost. This revised program is now in its fifth year of operation and the people of the area seem to be happy with it, although it makes their tax rates higher.

Case Number Six—Riverview

The metropolitan community of Riverview encompasses a large area which surrounds a city school district located within the same county. Riverview school district has witnessed unusual population and pupil growth for the past twelve years. Naval- and shipyards are owned by the United States government in this area, and, within this school district, there are several military installations which also belong to the federal government. The population not only grows but continues to shift within Riverview school district.

So much of the land in the school district is owned by the national government that financing instructional and school capital-outlay programs would be impossible from tax revenue from privately owned property. This district qualified, however, for the payments to the local board of education as obligations of the federal government arising from the non-taxable status of federally owned property, such property having been taxed locally before it was acquired by the federal government. The loss of tax revenues can reduce the amount of local funds available for schools to such an extent that financing public schools would be impossible.

Should Public-School Funds Be Spent for Nonpublic Schools?

Nonpublic schools must be considered an important part of the nation's educational resources. They serve millions of American pupils each year. Nonpublic elementary- and secondary-school enrollments have steadily increased since the turn of the century. In 1900 the nonpublic-school enrollment accounted for approximately 8 per cent of the total elementary and secondary enrollment; in 1953–54, they enrolled 13.08 per cent. If this trend continues, the U.S. Office of Education estimates that by 1965 the nonpublic elementary and secondary enrollment will be 6,840,000, or 14.60 per cent of the total elementary and secondary enrollment in the continental United States.

A nonpublic school is one under the immediate control of a private individual or organization and is usually supported by private funds rather than by public funds raised by taxation. This type of school may be operated on a profit or a nonprofit basis. Nonpublic schools are subject to regulatory controls exercised by the state, but, generally, the states are not concerned with private schools beyond establishing certain minimum standards. With few exceptions, the policy of state legislatures has been to encourage private effort in education.

The reasons for and against the spending of public funds for nonpublic education have been discussed by a number of authorities.[2] The following points are commonly made in opposition to the use of public funds for the support of nonpublic schools:

1. The First Amendment to the federal Constitution provides for complete separation of church and state.

2. Providing public funds for separate schools set up for religious groups or on a racial basis is an expensive and wasteful procedure.

[2] See National Education Association, Research Division, "The State and Sectarian Education," *Research Bulletin,* 34: 179–207, The Association, Washington, D.C., December, 1956; and Madaline K. Remmlein, *The Law of Local Public School Administration,* McGraw-Hill Book Company, Inc., New York, 1953, pp. 213–238.

3. If citizens do decide to grant financial support to non-public schools, the interest of the citizens who prefer to have their children attend public schools would need special protection.

4. Most state constitutions forbid the use of public funds for sectarian purposes.

5. The majority of the courts of the several states have held that direct appropriations to nonpublic schools are unconstitutional.

6. The use of nonschool revenue for direct aid to sectarian educational is unconstitutional.

The following points are commonly made in favor of the spending of public-school funds for nonpublic schools:

1. Other nations provide aid to nonpublic schools.

2. Nonpublic schools are exempt from taxation, which is really a sufficient precedent for governmental aid.

3. Legislatures have usually encouraged nonpublic schools.

4. The Supreme Court has upheld the practice of supplying free textbooks to both public and nonpublic-school pupils. (The books are furnished to the children and not to nonpublic schools, per se.)

5. Parents who send their children to nonpublic schools are subject to a kind of double taxation in that they must also support the local schools.

6. Transportation of parochial-school pupils at public expense has been held by the Supreme Court as not violating the First Amendment to the federal Constitution, even though most state courts do hold that this violates state constitutional provisions.

7. Health services should be provided to both public and nonpublic schools, in order to safeguard the health of our citizens.

Pupil-assignment laws, passed by some southern states to perpetuate segregation, contain clauses to provide tuition grants to public-school pupils, a trend which could also promote the cause of tuition grants for nonpublic schools as well. The relationship of the state and public education to nonpublic education has been widely discussed in recent years, and undoubtedly other court rulings and new interpretations will be appearing. But government aid to nonpublic schools is still a matter of controversy, and, other than transportation of pupils and providing free textbooks and health services, there actually has been little money from public-school funds spent for nonpublic schools.

Case Number Seven illustrates how the Supreme Court of the United States can make decisions that affect local school districts in matters of aid to nonpublic schools. Since the state involved in this case did not argue violation of the First Amendment to the federal Constitution, the ruling was based on another principle.

Case Number Eight illustrates that public schools may rent parochial-school buildings and use them for public education, as long as curricular control remains with the local board of education.

Case Number Seven—Edison Township

The school district known as Edison Township became involved in a controversy concerning transportation of nonpublic school pupils to their school. The heart of the issue involved the right of the local school board to use tax money to reimburse parents for the transportation expense of children attending certain parochial schools. This case was appealed to the United States Supreme Court, but the state concerned did argue the question of whether transportation of nonpublic schools at public expense violates the First Amendment to the federal Constitution.

Making transportation facilities available to pupils attending parochial schools was compared by the court with police and fire protection offered to all schools, and, as such, a legitimate concern of local government. The Edison Township board of education appropriated money to reimburse parents for the transportation costs they had expended in getting their children to school by common carrier.

Although the United States Supreme Court has ruled that the First Amendment does not prohibit transporting parochial-school pupils at public expense, the local constitutionality of this practice has been upheld by only three states, and at least one state has distinguished between the school fund of the state and other public funds.

Case Number Eight—Andersonville

The school district of Andersonville encompasses the city itself and much of the surrounding area, having twelve high schools and more than thirty elementary schools. The board of education is composed of five members elected by popular vote. The superintendent is appointed by the board and, in the present case, was serving his fifth year in this position.

During the Christmas holidays, one of the largest high-school buildings was destroyed by fire, creating an almost overnight need for a school plant to house 800 pupils. The board of education and superintendent considered all possibilities and finally agreed to rent the local Catholic Church building, which was near the location of the old building and the center of population for the particular school. The church authorities were invited to meet with the superintendent and the board of education. An amicable agreement was reached and put in writing. Later, the superintendent's office was crowded with angry parents who objected that the renting of church buildings was illegal and who further contended that attending classes in these buildings would expose their children to Catholic doctrine.

The superintendent and board of education held an open meeting and invited all citizens of the attendance area. They explained that school would be held in a parochial building but that the school would be under public control and thus was a legally operated public school. It was pointed out that public education can be conducted in a parochial building if the board of education has control of the schools, and if no religious tenets are taught. Rent paid to a church for the use of its building under these circumstances is generally not considered aid.

The church building was used for the remainder of the school year. The local board made rental payments from public-school funds, and the school remained under the supervision and control of the school district. The following year the pupils returned to a new plant which replaced the building that had been destroyed by fire.

Should Public-School Funds Be Expended to Improve School Public-Relations Programs?

One very important factor that some school administrators overlook is that, more directly than almost any other public enterprise, the nation's schools belong to and are operated by the people of each community. Therefore, if the public schools are to be public in a real sense, it is important that the people share in the basic decisions which affect them and their children. Obviously, since the schools belong to the people and since the people establish and maintain them, there can be no doubt about the right of the people to know all they desire to know about what the schools are doing. These rights are clearly made firm in laws governing finance, records, and the like. The science of education requires that the schools of a democracy be kept very close to the people; in fact, that the people participate actively in making the schools. This becomes an aspect of public relations for which school administrators are responsible. Besides social, legal, and scientific justifications for the recognition of this function, there is also the very practical necessity of keeping on good working terms with the people.

The development of education in the United States depends, to a large extent, upon the attitudes of the public and its willingness and ability to provide the necessary finances. As long as education justifies itself in the minds of those who are instrumental in financing it, the financing will continue, and the public will generally be eager to take part in strengthening the school program.

How much money a school system should budget for public-relations personnel, media, and services is a problem that has not had enough study. Accurate figures on the cost of operating a public-relations program are difficult to obtain because many school systems charge parts of the costs to various other departments or sections of the budget. Some of the budgeted tax money will be spent directly or indirectly for school public relations, since all certified and noncertified school personnel are public-relations agents in their own right. Many of the activities of the schools, such as special-day programs, exhibits, extracurricular activities, promotions, commencement exercises, bulletins to the home, and annual reports will be paid for from public tax funds. Most of the services of the school system, such as guidance, health, transportation, and specialized classes, are likewise paid for from public-school funds.

The cost of such public relations will vary from year to year, depending upon the scope of the program and what the school district wishes to do.

It is still possible to find a few professional educators who have little faith in the practice of spending tax funds for public-relations programs for the public schools. It is their contention that advertising in daily newspapers in return for publication of the news of the school district is, for example, undesirable, because the public schools are social institutions which should serve the needs of the community rather than any selfish or commercial advantages. Others fear that administrators will use the money budgeted for public relations to further their own selfish goals. In addition, there are states where it is illegal to budget public-school funds for public-relations purposes.

In general, school boards have not seen fit to provide a budget and sufficient funds to conduct adequate public-relations programs. Costs are often charged elsewhere, and details of expenditures are not known. A planned program calls for information on the amount of money which will be available so it can be put to the best advantage. Financial support for the various agencies should come from the regular school budget. This budget should be adequate for the effective use of all the agencies of a public-relations program.

The foundation of public willingness to support education lies in community attitudes toward public education. A school, perhaps more than most public institutions, owes its existence to the community. All of the people are stockholders in the school enterprise, and they have the same desire and right to be kept informed concerning their public possession as have stockholders in private business.

Making a school budget is a technical task that should be

performed only by those with professional preparation in school finance. Sound budgeting is not merely a throwing together of casual estimates or expressing in monetary terms the good intentions of the administrator and the board. A school budget is a systematized statement which forecasts the expenditures and the revenues of the school district during a stated period of time.

The ideal school budget contains three parts: (1) the work plan, which is a definite statement of educational policies and program; (2) the spending plan, which is a translation of the accepted policies into proposed expenditures; and (3) the financing plan, which proposes means for meeting the cost of the educational needs. The educational plan should be well developed, since it forms the basis for the spending and financing programs. Ideally, a well-planned budget would be completely spent by the end of the fiscal year.

The effect on school public relations of the way budgeting is carried on is partly dependent upon how much information the community receives. If there is a broad program of public information, budgeting can be an important asset in helping to build confidence and understanding within the local community.

Case Number Nine illustrates what is possible when an enlightened superintendent and board of education use public-school funds for public relations in a constructive way.

Case Number Ten gives an example of what can happen when a school administrator uses money budgeted for public relations to advance his own selfish goals.

Case Number Nine—McKeesville

Although above average in terms of wealth, for many years the school district of McKeesville had operated on a low expenditure per child for instruction. The city and its adjoining area had grown in population steadily for ten years. The superintendent who served during the ten years of this growth retired. During his tenure, two bond issues for new buildings had been defeated, and school taxes had increased very little —not nearly enough to care for the increased population adequately.

The new superintendent, appointed by the board, visited the State Department of Education and found that McKeesville was one of the many school districts that did not budget the legal ½ per cent for school public relations. The new superintendent and the board remedied this situation, and the money was spent for various media to help citizens better to understand their schools. Effective results were obtained through establishment of a radio station in the central high school. The radius of this little station was about thirty-five miles; in other words, it reached about 98 per cent of the people in the school district. Very few teachers, administrators, or other persons went "on the air." Instead, the students themselves explained classwork, school services, co-curricular services, and the work of the school in general. For the next seven years the superintendent and board were able to increase school taxes each year. The school district of McKeesville is now well known as one adequately supported by the local citizens.

Case Number Ten—Super County

Located in the middle of a large farming belt, Super County is inhabited largely by middle-class people, who are, for the most part, salaried workers. Industry in the county is limited to one small plastics factory. School taxes at the local level come mostly from property taxes. The assessment ratio varies widely within the county. The amount of money spent for each pupil in average daily attendance for instruction is approximately one half the national average. The school program lacked numerous offerings which would have been helpful to most of its pupils. In fact, many citizens of the community felt that Super County was not making enough effort to support education.

Although the school district budgeted more than ½ per cent of its total operational budget for public relations, there was little evidence that the school and community had a close working relationship. The superintendent used the public-relations fund to publish a monthly newsletter which was distributed to all certified and noncertified school personnel and to the parents of all school children within the district. The superintendent's name generally appeared several times on each page, and lavish praise was often showered upon him in articles about accomplishments of the school system. Very little information about instruction, curriculum, and individual achievements was carried. The superintendent also bought radio time each week for school news.

When a full-time public-relations director was employed and began to give credits to the board of education, the PTA, the faculties, and the community residents for school improvements, the superintendent asked that the public-relations director have all manuscripts for district-wide publication come through his office for editing before being made public. The self-centered and insecure superintendent became so hostile that the director resigned at the end of the year. The director made known his reasons for resignation in a letter to the board. The board requested that the superintendent resign, which he did.

Questions for Discussion

Case Number One

1. What is a fiscally dependent school district?
2. Should a board of education present its budget to another authority for approval? Why?

Case Number Two

3. What part did fiscal independence play in the case of Blackberry Hill?
4. What was the issue in this case? As superintendent, what would you have done?

Case Number Three

5. What was wrong with the local tax structure in Beaconville?
6. Assume that you are chairman of the school board. What action would you take?

Case Number Four

7. What was the problem in Smokeyville?
8. How was this problem resolved?

Case Number Five

9. To what extent are controls attached to federal aid to vocational education?
10. How can these controls be avoided? Did the school board act wisely in this case?

Case Number Six

11. How does nontaxable property belonging to the federal government affect the local school district?
12. To what extent does the federal government reimburse the local districts in lieu of taxes?

Case Number Seven

13. Upon what data was this decision based?

14. Does the First Amendment prohibit transporting parochial pupils at public expense? What conclusions may be drawn from this case?

Case Number Eight

15. Can the public schools rent parochial-school buildings and use them for public education?

16. Can religious tenets be taught in public schools?

Case Number Nine

17. What is the problem in this case?

18. Did the board of education and the superintendent act wisely? What conclusions can be drawn from this case?

Case Number Ten

19. Evaluate the actions of the superintendent.

20. Did any improvements result?

21. What action would you have taken had you been superintendent?

Selected Readings

American Association of School Administrators, *Public Relations for America's Schools,* Twenty-eighth Yearbook, The Association, Washington, D.C., 1950, Chap. X.

Beach, Fred, and Will, Robert F., *The State and Nonpublic Schools,* Office of Education, U.S. Department of Health, Education, and Welfare, Washington, D.C., 1958, Chaps. I, III.

Burke, Arvid J., *Financing Public Schools in the United States,* Harper & Brothers, New York, 1957, Chaps. VIII, IX.

Educational Policies Commission, *The Unique Function of Education in American Democracy,* The Commission, Washington, D.C., 1937.

Fowlkes, John Guy, and Watson, George E., "School Finance and Local Planning," *Studies in Educational Administration,* Midwest Administration Center, University of Chicago, Chicago, 1957.

Hunt, Herold G., and Pierce, Paul R., *The Practice of School Administration,* Houghton Mifflin Company, Boston, 1958, Chap. XVI.

Johns, R. L., *The Property Tax and Public School Financing,* NEA Legislative Commission, Washington, D.C., 1958.

Johns, R. L., and Morphet, E. L., editors, *Problems and Issues in Public School Finance,* Bureau of Publications, Teachers College, Columbia University, 1952, Chaps. VIII, IX.

Jones, James J., *An Analysis and Summary of the Significant Research Findings Concerning Some Problems and Issues of School-Community Relations,* unpublished doctor's dissertation, Indiana University, Bloomington, 1952.

Mort, Paul R., and Reusser, Walter C., *Public School Finance,* McGraw-Hill Book Company, Inc., New York, 1951.

National Education Association, Research Division, "The State and Sectarian Education," *Research Bulletin,* Vol. 34, No. 4, pp. 179–207, The Association, Washington, D.C., December, 1956.

Remmlein, Madaline K., *The Law of Local Public School Administration,* McGraw-Hill Book Company, Inc., New York, 1953, Chap. VIII.

ISSUES DEALING WITH THE SCHOOL PLANT

4.

THE primary functions of a school plant are to house the children and to facilitate the educational program. To carry out this role, the school should be safe, healthful, attractive, efficient, economical, and functional. In designing a school plant, one must consider the amount of housing needed currently and in the near future, factors dependent upon the scope and quality of the community's educational program. The community's educational philosophy must also be considered, as this will give some evidence of the extent to which the school will be used for community activities as well as school functions. The amount of money the community can afford or is willing to spend for school buildings and equipment must be agreed upon.

Physical environment probably contributes as much toward the success of a pupil in school as any other single factor. Perhaps the best educational environment is planned around and for children. Since so many of the youth's waking hours are spent in school, the environment for learning should welcome the child instead of repelling him. School buildings should be built and equipped so that seeing, hearing, sitting, and other physical aspects of work are accomplished with a minimum of strain and fatigue. Thus pupils can reserve a maximum amount of energy for purposeful learning. Although a school building may be the largest single piece of teaching equipment, it should be a thing of functional beauty.

Public relations are involved in planning a school plant and its use, maintenance, repair, and financing. The major considerations in this chapter are given to citizen participation in the planning of school plants, designing school plants for community use, the use of the school plant and facilities by outside groups, and who should do the repair work? How well the administrator plans for and treats such issues will determine to a high degree how successful his public-relations program will be.

Should Citizens Participate in the Planning of School Plants?

There are people who contend that lay citizens have no part to play in planning school buildings. They believe that laymen know too little about the nature of school plants and the type of school program a building must house and that the professional staff, the board of education, and the architect should be free to do the job without outside interference. Some contend that citizen participation, even if desirable, would delay the planning and construction of buildings. Others argue that the community has no real desire to participate because its members are busy performing their daily tasks for a livelihood, and that community support will be the same regardless of who does the planning. Some citizens feel that they have no business suggesting to professional people the kind or type of buildings to be erected. A relatively small number of citizens may not be interested one way or another.

The arguments presented against citizen participation in the planning of school buildings have little foundation. Granted that laymen know little or nothing about school buildings, opportunity to participate might increase their insight and understanding about school-construction problems. Likewise, a good professional staff might welcome suggestions from persons other than professionals. The contention that citizen participation delays the planning and development of school plants frequently portrays the lack of advance planning being done by some school officials. If plans are begun early enough, the extra time consumed in involving citizens will be almost negligible; but, more to the point, who is going to pay the bill? Should the purchasers of a building not have a voice in its construction? If favorable results are to be accomplished, planning the school building should be shared by all who will be affected by its construction, from educationists to taxpayers.

The local board of education has the legal responsibility to provide the needed school plant and facilities, but the superintendent is responsible for initiating, directing, and supervising school-plant planning. Although lay citizens of a community cannot decide technical problems of school-plant planning or make decisions concerning the interrelation of school program and school plant, they can participate with the superintendent and board in arriving at a general concept of the type of school which the community wants. This does not mean that every man's neighbor has to be leaning over the conference table when the school building committee and the architect discuss the building program. It does mean that, step by step, the major decisions should be explained and publicized and have the general support of local citizens. All laymen who participate in the planning should know that they are working in an advisory capacity and that the local board of education makes the final decision.

The enlistment of citizens in lay groups and special committees for solution of school building problems will make a difference in the support secured for building programs. If citizen participation is to work effectively, the superintendent and board of education must be convinced of its value and be prepared to give honest and full consideration to committee recommendations. In cooperative planning, neither the board of education nor the school administrators give up any of their legal and moral rights and objectives. The committees should have access to all data and have consultant help available when needed, but they should be made aware that their services are advisory.

The value to the school of citizen participation in developing school building programs is self-evident. Lay groups may possess many kinds of knowledge and experience useful to professional planners and may well have more intimate knowledge of the community and its needs than do professional educators. Perhaps no group is better qualified to provide information about selected aspects of the community than are its local citizens. In the final analysis, identification of the community with the building program through citizen participation promotes community acceptance and adoption of the entire school program.

The following cases illustrate two kinds of citizen participation in planning school buildings. The first case depicts the leadership of a supervising principal who is capable of organizing lay citizens for such planning. The second case illustrates how lack of leadership on the part of school officials in a case involving citizen participation can lead to serious problems.

Case Number One—Lovejoy Hill

Under the leadership of the supervising principal, this suburban community had citizens, teachers, building employees, and pupils participate in the total planning procedure for the construction of a new junior-senior high school. A citizen committee of more than twenty members was appointed by the board of education to study the community and school needs. This committee was fairly representative of the community. It was aided by parents, pupils, and teachers and was led by the supervising principal. It also had an architect as consultant. Organized visits were made to nearby school buildings, and their programs and plants were studied carefully. Many significant data were collected. After more than a year of continuous study, the central committee made its report to the board of education. Immediately, the board of education called a community meeting. Citizens were called upon for suggestions, and drawings and specifications growing out of these suggestions were recommended for acceptance. The new school, when finally completed, was a source of pride and joy for the entire community.

Later, a bond issue which had been twice defeated passed by a large majority, and the committee continued in existence to study other problems and school needs. This was the same community which had changed principals frequently and had formerly been made up of several factions.

Case Number Two—Button County

The rural county of Button encompasses less than 800 square miles of territory. It has one village of approximately 5,000 population near the center of the county. Agriculture is the principal activity of the county and its major source of income. Although the total school population has grown less than ½ per cent in two decades, the county has a school-plant shortage which dates back more than ten years.

The State Department of Education had made two building surveys, at five-year intervals, both of which culminated in a recommendation that the county's eight small high schools be consolidated. The superintendent and the board of education took no action except to discuss the matter with a few leading citizens. A self-appointed citizen group, led by a minister, a physician, and a farmer, opposed the recommendation of the State Department of Education. As one member of the group put it, "We don't want our children riding buses for hours to and from school and we don't want our children attending some super-high school." The group met at various villages and small communities within the county to disseminate their objections to the proposed consolidation.

After two bond issues had been defeated, the board of education and superintendent finally brought in consultants from the nearby state university and invited the citizen committee to meet with them and study the data collected by the group. After several open meetings, the citizens agreed to vote for a school building program that would give them one central high school. Consolidation was finally effected, but only after lack of constructive leadership had allowed a headstrong citizen group to frustrate, for years, this much-needed reform.

Should School Plants Be Designed for Community Use?

Almost every administrator constantly hears the word "economize." Unfortunately, in too many instances what is thought to be economy is actually false economy. Cutbacks which are supposed to save money may actually handicap and reduce the efficiency of the program and lead eventually to even greater expenditure. It is true, however, that when school plants are designed for community as well as school use, additional cost is involved.

There are many factors which must be given careful consideration if the community is to use the school plant—for example, location of facilities to be used by the community, distribution of heat, adequate storage space for equipment, special service features, and extra toilet facilities. Also, after completion of the plant, extra custodial care will be needed to keep buildings clean, additional repairs will be necessary, and extra supervision on the part of school personnel will be required. There will be problems, too, connected with scheduling community activities, so as not to interfere with schoolwork, and with decisions as to what groups may and may not use the facilities.

Despite such drawbacks, community use of school plants has much in its favor. School buildings that are designed for community use can be used not only for public meetings that concern the schools but also for social gatherings of neighborhood groups. It is important that citizens and taxpayers become well acquainted with their schools. The taxpayer who knows his school intimately rarely grudges reasonable levies for educational purposes.

There are many ways in which school plants can be used as community centers. They may be used for gym classes for adults, recreational clubs, study groups, philanthropic organizations, civic-improvement leagues, discussion groups, and other social gatherings. Adult classes can be developed, and the school can promote preschool study groups for mothers and provide playground service during summer months. It can provide a forum for study of local social and economic problems.

The cafeteria, the gymnasium, and the auditorium should be almost as familiar to patrons as to school children. When citizens use the school buildings and come to know them intimately, it is not likely that they will fail to be interested in what the children do there. Moreover, they will tend to take an active interest in proper maintenance of buildings and grounds and in enlarging the facilities of the school.

The school plant is a very vital agency in the social interpretation program, and, properly used, can stimulate and improve public contacts with the school as a social institution.

Recognition and physical provision for the reception and comfort of visitors will do much to attract them. Educators have been advocating for years that the school plant be designed to provide not only for educational needs but also for many of the social, civic, recreational, and cultural needs of the entire community.

In many instances, inefficient utilization of public buildings and duplications of expensive building materials can be avoided when community programs are held in school buildings that provide adequate facilities. Extra money and better planning are likely to accompany efforts on the part of school people to have the school serve as a community center.

Case Number Three indicates how the structure of a community may change over a period of time and how the bias of local people may unnecessarily restrict the use of a building designed for community use.

Case Number Four illustrates the advantages of intelligent planning of a school plant for community use.

Case Number Three—Buttsville

The Buttsville consolidated-high-school plant was designed for community use when it was built. During the past decade this village has become urbanized to a high degree, bringing an influx of people with a variety of religious beliefs. Although originally the community was composed largely of people of Baptist faith, at least seven other denominations are now represented.

Buttsville school authorities had permitted and encouraged the citizens to participate in planning a building which could be used by the community. The facilities to be used by the community were located in one section of the building and included extra toilet and service facilities, additional features which had cost the community extra tax dollars.

Urbanization of the community brought numerous requests from groups other than the Baptists to use the school. A group representing the Catholic faith, whose church was in the process of being built, requested permission to use the school gymnasium for mass until its church could be completed. Although the Baptist church had been given permission to use the gymnasium temporarily for services when its church burned, the board flatly denied the request of the Catholics. The board of education met with a few unorganized community groups to discuss the matter and then passed a rule that only the older and more "stable" groups within the community should use the plant. Board members based their position on the assumption that newcomers to the community did not understand local conditions.

Case Number Four—Big Town

The school superintendent and the board of education of Big Town school district were involved in identifying the school-building needs of the district and in planning a central high school. Owing to the fact that so many of the activities of the community took place on the school campus, many under poor conditions, the board decided, upon the recommendation of the superintendent, to plan the central-high-school plant in a manner which would meet both educational and community needs. The superintendent noted that few additional facilities over and above those commonly found in a modern school building would be needed to take care of many of the community activities now being held under difficult circumstances. Further, it was pointed out that some rooms could be used by both school and community.

The board of education appointed a representative citizen committee of thirty members to work with the professional staff, school employees, and consultants to study the school-building needs.

The study was conducted continuously for almost twelve months. The consultants and the professional staff worked as a part of the group. When the final recommendations of the committee were submitted to the board one year later, the board accepted more than 95 per cent of its suggestions. The bond issue which followed was voted in by the largest majority in the history of the school system. In recognizing and providing for the needs of community members, this school system has done much to promote good will.

When Should the School Plant and Facilities Be Used by Outside Groups?

Although, during the past two decades, there has been a well-defined movement toward making the school the center of community life, this does not imply that the public has freedom to do as it pleases with school plants. The primary use of the school plant is for the school's pupils, and school buildings should be used by the general public only during the evenings or at other times when schoolwork will not be hindered.

Every school board, whether of a large or a small school system, should adopt rules and regulations for community use of school property. These regulations should prescribe the method of obtaining permission to use the property, the time of use, conditions of use, and the fees, if any, which must be paid for the use. If the school plant and facilities are not scheduled for use, there will be conflicts and misunderstandings, and poor relationships may develop. A set of rules and regulations reduces to routine much of the work of letting school property and gives greater assurance that all groups of the community will be treated alike. Without such guides, school officials are open to accusation of partiality.

Legal restrictions may also govern the extended use of school buildings for other than school purposes. Most of the states have laws providing for the community use of school buildings. Within these limitations, it is commonly agreed that local school authorities are the custodians of school property and have the right to grant or withhold use of the public schools for other than public-school purposes.

In theory, public-school property is merely held in trust for the state by local authorities, and the legislature may authorize its use for any purpose not prohibited by the constitution, but there are so many conflicting opinions and statutes on the use of public-school property that conclusions are difficult to draw. For example, state statutes, as well as the courts, are divided as to the use of school buildings for religious exercises; for social, fraternal, and political meetings; and for private and public dances. Boards of education should, of course, not permit use of school facilities for private gain or for purposes in opposition to the public good. The superintendent and the professional staff must be alert, courageous, and effective in opposing the attempts of pressure groups to control or circumvent school programs and policies.

Community use of school buildings has greatly increased with the expansion of adult-education programs, the development of emergency and evening schools, and the increase of leisure time available to our society. University- and college-extension divisions use public-school buildings in order to make readily available their vast resources to the general public. Libraries use the schools as lending branches in order to facilitate public use of their facilities. The federal government, particularly in agricultural areas, makes use of school facilities to spread the benefits of agricultural, social, and health research. The school playground can provide a place for weekend, summer, after-school, and evening recreational programs for both youth and adults. The school also becomes a meeting place for selected youth organizations.

In the school community center, adults and young people are brought into a common environment for recreational activities, which helps to promote a good understanding between various age groups. An educational program, in addition to its other community benefits, helps young people assimilate the idea that learning is a lifelong process, not something that stops with the termination of formal schooling. The school-community center may become a strong influence in bringing the interests of adults and youth together through sportsmen's clubs, garden clubs, dancing clubs, athletic contests, and other social activities.

Teachers should join in school-community activities as participants, spectators, or leaders and should give encouragement to the center by working on committees, participating in activities, and supporting the programs.

School-plant facilities represent a substantial investment by the taxpayer, and the administrators and boards of education who make them available to the public are also making a significant contribution to better school public relations.

Case Number Five illustrates how unsupervised community activity on school property can work hardship on the pupils of a school. Case Number Six indicates the value to a community of adult classes held in school buildings.

Case Number Five—Spotmore

The village of Spotmore has a combination elementary and high school which includes grades one through twelve located on the same campus. A large number of the children are transported to Spotmore from the surrounding territory, and the total enrollment is approximately 500. The elementary pupils are housed in one building and the high-school pupils in another. The toilet facilities for the high-school pupils are located in an adjoining building and also in the gymnasium.

The principal of the combined schools was in his first year of service when he discovered that community groups were using the gymnasium, the shop, and the lunchroom without his being consulted. He went to the superintendent to learn the county's policy in regard to the use of school facilities. Since the superintendent and members of the board of education had been elected by popular vote, they did not wish to get into a conflict with out-of-school groups who might hinder their re-election, so the principal was told to handle the problem on his own, but to avoid trouble.

A retired minister took a group of Boy Scouts into the gymnasium the following week for a monthly meeting. The boys skated on the newly sanded and polished gymnasium floor and filled commodes with toilet tissue. The next morning the high-school pupils were forced to use the toilets in the elementary building because the high-school toilets would not work. Repair of the toilets and the gymnasium floor cost over $300. The board of education hesitatingly paid the bill.

The superintendent and the board invited the principal and his faculty to draw up policies concerning the use of Spotmore school buildings, and the county board of education, with a few modifications, adopted the policies. Although a number of parents and citizens at first objected to the change, once the policies were understood, the citizens developed a more responsible attitude toward the school authorities, the board of education, and the use of school property.

Case Number Six—Keithville

Keithville, a city of over 300,000 population, has a modern school system. Professional employees, the board of education, and members of the community work together to improve the school program. The district is long established, and its buildings, although well kept, reflect much use. The central-high-school building is a three-story brick structure located on a small lot in the center of the city and is over twenty years old. Its parking area is small and restricted. The city has grown in all directions since the erection of the building, but it remains near the center of the school district and is accessible to many patrons and citizens.

The state university conducted extension classes two nights a week in the central-high-school plant, offering classes for credit and noncredit. The school board paid for the utilities and custodial care in order that the local public could take advantage of the university's resources. Likewise, the federal government used the building to teach teachers of agriculture and to give "on-the-job training" to veterans. Other adult programs, including trade and mechanical training, were conducted by the school system in the afternoon and evenings. Frequent use was made of the school plant by the parent-teacher association, mothers' club, Red Cross, and various community clubs. The facilities of the high school are used almost around the clock, but adherence to strict policy rules for community use of the plant prevents any interference with the needs of the students and contributes much to good public relations.

Should School Employees or Outside Contractors Do the Repair Work?

It is important that the school plant be kept in good repair and look attractive at all times. Depreciation of a school building begins the minute the building is completed and turned over to school authorities. Repairs and replacements are essential in any school plant, however well constructed. The school building plays a major role in the instructional program, and it also plays an important part in the public relations of the school. Attractive, clean foyers, corridors, and classrooms and good landscaping can contribute much to public acceptance of the school and its program.

Expenditures for repairs and replacements of school plants vary widely. In a large school system maintenance may be big business, whereas in a small system a lesser amount of repair may be necessary. Irrespective of the size of the school, the climatic conditions, or the geographic location, it is necessary to have someone responsible for discovering needed repairs and to report them promptly to the administration or the board of education.

The most common arguments in support of school employees doing maintenance work for the school system are as follows: School employees get to know the local school buildings inside and out and are naturally better informed about the plant's physical needs than are persons from the outside. The employees of the school system have an opportunity to learn the needs of the professional staff. Regular employees of a school district will need less supervision than will outside persons. Use of local school employees can reduce costs; regular employees of a school system develop maintenance skills and know-how through their on-the-job experience. Of course, school systems may need to engage workmen on a contract or on an hourly basis for special repair jobs, but many repairs can easily be made by the janitor or school custodian.

Common arguments in support of outside contractors doing the school repairs are as follows: There are seasons of the year when the school employees are so busy that they cannot handle the work to be done. Many repair jobs require the special tools, equipment, and skills which regular employees may not possess.

In general, school systems may have their employees do what they can best do and have other repairs let out on bids to contractors. Each school system will need to study its own situation before acting.

Case Number Seven illustrates what can happen when a school system depends almost entirely upon outside contractors to do the school repairs. It also points up the need for having a repair policy and someone to help it operate. Case Number Eight illustrates what can happen when the local school system depends entirely upon the school employees to make repairs.

Case Number Seven—Oyster Bay

Oyster Bay school district is located in a fairly isolated area. The school system has a pupil population of 5,000. It is not large enough or wealthy enough to employ full-time workmen to make school repairs. Necessary repairs are, more often than not, made by a contractor from a distant city, and there is generally a time lapse between the discovery of the necessity for repairs and the letting of contracts for the job.

One day the head custodian of the largest school plant within the Oyster Bay system discovered a leaky classroom roof. Although the need to repair the roof was discovered in December, securing outside contractors resulted in a delay of nearly six months before the work was begun. By this time, not only did the roof need repairing but also the ceiling and two walls of a classroom had to be replastered and painted. Earlier repair could have been made for a fraction of the final cost if school employees had been trained to do work of this type.

Case Number Eight—Fort Bacon

Located in the center of an industrial area, Fort Bacon city school system is considered to be one of the best in the state. The city's population exceeds 400,000, and the school district is large in terms of square miles. Usually, during the summer months, the custodial staff is organized into work groups to make repairs and replacements in the school plant. These workmen are employed on an annual basis. Many of them have special skills needed for the summer repairs, but others do not. The Fort Bacon school board seldom uses other than custodial personnel to do its repair work.

One summer the school custodians had to replace a worn-out heating system in one of the high-school gymnasiums. Tools and other equipment had to be rented from local heating and ventilating companies, and, after several false starts and much hard work, the workmen finally made the installation. In the fall, when school opened, the new heating and ventilating system failed to work satisfactorily, and the board of education had to contract for a regular heating and ventilating company to make the necessary adjustments. Money and time had been lost because unskilled labor had been put to work on a task requiring professional help.

Questions for Discussion

Case Number One

1. To what do you attribute the success or lack of success of citizen participation in the planning of the school plant?

2. What can be learned from this example that would be helpful in promoting school public relations?

Case Number Two

3. What was the difficulty with citizen planning in this case?

4. How would you avoid the pitfalls found here? Explain.

Case Number Three

5. How do you account for the change in attitude of the community toward the school? Is the change defensible?

6. As an administrator, how would you go about seeking a solution to this problem?

Case Number Four

7. What factors are significant in planning a school plant for community use as well as for school use? Were these criteria met in this case?

8. What do you consider to be the strong points in terms of public relations in this case?

Case Number Five

9. What criteria should be considered by a board when establishing policy in regard to the use of school buildings by outside groups?

10. How can board policy in regard to use of school property by outside groups be administered in such way as to promote school public relations?

Case Number Six

11. To what extent should the community use the school buildings? How can conflicts with school activities be resolved?

12. Should the board of education spend local funds to promote the use of its buildings by outside groups? Why?

Case Number Seven

13. What factors should be considered in deciding who is to do the repairs? How can costs be estimated in such cases?

14. What basic repair policies need revising?

Case Number Eight

15. What criteria should be considered in deciding when to use outside contractors for repairs?

16. What suggestion can you make concerning the necessary steps to improve this system of repairs and replacements?

17. Discuss what you consider to be the essential elements involved in school public relations in this case.

Selected Readings

American Association of School Administrators, *American School Buildings,* Twenty-seventh Yearbook, The Association, Washington, D.C., 1949, Chap. II.

Creighton, Thomas, "Use Your Building Program to Build Friends," *Nation's Schools,* **34**: 37–39, November, 1944.

Essex, Don L., "Planning the School Building for Community Use," *Review of Educational Research,* **18**: 28–31, February, 1948.

Herrick, John H., *et al., From School Program to School Plant,* Henry Holt and Company, Inc., New York, 1956, Chap. 1.

Hunt, Herold C., and Pierce, Paul R., *The Practice of School Administration,* Houghton Mifflin Company, Boston, 1958, Chap. XIX.

Linn, Henry H., *School Business Administration,* The Ronald Press Company, New York, 1956, Chap. 13.

National Society for the Study of Education, *Citizen Cooperation for Better Public Schools,* Fifty-third Yearbook of the NSSE, Pt. I, University of Chicago Press, Chicago, 1954.

Seagers, Paul W., *Community Participation in School Building Planning,* unpublished doctor's dissertation, Teachers College, Columbia University, New York, 1950.

Sumption, Merle R., and Landis, Jack L., *Planning Functional School Buildings,* Harper & Brothers, New York, 1957, Chap. 3.

ISSUES DEALING WITH
PERSONNEL ADMINISTRATION

5.

$\mathbf{O}$F THE many important duties school administrators perform, one which has far-reaching effects is the way they manage the job of personnel administration. This task involves the handling of problems which arise from the various relationships of the school staff. Personnel administration is a process carried on by many persons. It is dependent upon superintendents, principals, supervisors, teachers, and school-board members who are in positions of responsibility to contribute to the attainment of the objectives of the school.

In order to bring about conditions under which effective learning is most likely to take place, administrators must engage in a variety of activities. Included in this array of functions are the formulation and development of well-defined personnel policies that can be defended and administered with wisdom and justice.

Administrators should bear in mind that good morale on the part of teachers is directly related to clearly defined personnel policies and procedures. The social and professional climate within the school system needs careful and constant consideration. Unhappy or discontented teachers can spend time and effort, that they should be devoting to their daily work, in fighting an unpopular administration.

The major purpose of this chapter is to treat factors of personnel administration such as merit salary schedules, in-service training, tenure, and faculty participation in policy development.

Should the Merit Salary Schedule Be Used for the Payment of Teachers?

One of the difficult problems faced today by school administrators and the teaching profession involves the controversy over the merit rating of teachers. In far too many instances there has been more heat than light—more emotional thinking and less critical study than are desirable. The controversy feeds on an abundance of professional literature and research, which seems to favor first one side and then the other, and is influenced by the general popularity of the single salary schedule with professional organizations and teachers.

The arguments for and against the merit salary schedule have been summarized by a number of authorities.[1] The major ones advanced in support of merit salary schedules are as follows:

1. Merit should be rewarded by paying each teacher according to the worth of his contribution.

[1] See B. J. Chandler and Paul V. Petty, *Personnel Management in School Administration,* World Book Company, Yonkers, N.Y., 1955; Chap. 8 in Willard Elsbree and Edmund Reutter, Jr., *Staff Personnel in the Public Schools,* Prentice-Hall, Inc., Englewood Cliffs, N.J., 1954; Chap. 6 in Albert L. Ayars, *Administering the People's Schools,* McGraw-Hill Book Co., Inc., New York, 1957; Chap. 7 in National Education Association, Research Division, *Reference on Teacher Rating and Evaluation,* November, 1955; and William A. McCall, *Measurement of Teacher Merit,* Publication No. 284, State Superintendent of Public Instruction, Raleigh, N.C., 1952.

2. Evaluation helps teachers to be alert and tends to reward the ambitious and creative and to penalize the laggards.

3. Merit rating can lead to higher maximum salary schedules since not everyone will reach the top of the scale at the same time.

4. Years of college preparation and teaching experience are inadequate criteria for a salary schedule.

5. Merit ratings are similar to wage practices established in industry and in government service.

6. Merit ratings appeal to taxpayers who have to finance the public schools.

7. Evaluation will be made regardless of whether it is planned evaluation or not—by teachers, administrators, pupils, parents, and the public.

8. Merit salary plans are "reward" programs for good teaching, *not* "penalty" programs to punish poor teaching.

9. Merit salary schedules attract and hold capable young minds in the teaching profession.

10. There are selected school systems that have merit salary schedules which work satisfactorily.

The chief arguments against merit rating in salary schedules are:

1. It is difficult to establish a merit pay plan when substandard salaries are paid and there is a shortage of teaching personnel.

2. Some of the most important aspects of teaching are the most difficult to examine and to rate objectively.

3. There is little, if any, conclusive evidence that merit rating improves those rated.

4. Many school systems throughout the nation have experimented with the merit rating type of salary schedule and have given it up.

5. Parents strenuously object to having some children taught by teachers who have a high rating while others are taught by teachers with a low rating.

6. The people who are to be rated are not always invited to take part in the development of plans, procedures, and operations of the merit schedule.

7. Merit ratings hinder professionalism by causing teachers to be hesitant about sharing ideas with their fellow teachers, whom they come to consider competitors rather than colleagues.

8. Existing rating devices frequently do not measure what they purport to measure, and often the ratings are unreliable.

The real test of merit pay plan lies in whether or not it improves the instructional program. This is a difficult test to make, but the school system must determine to what degree the merit principle is working for the benefit of school pupils. Administrators and others should keep open minds on the matter and should encourage, through research and experimentation, all efforts toward developing sound criteria, in addition to years of preparation and experience, for salary increases.

Case Number One illustrates an unsuccessful merit salary schedule. Case Number Two illustrates a generally successful one.

Case Number One—Lincoln

The school district of Lincoln encompasses a city and suburban areas. Many taxpayers complained that all teachers were paid the same, regardless of their abilities; they pointed out that workers in local industries were not all paid alike and that teachers, like local workers, should be rated for promotion and, when the situation warranted, for dismissal. One day the school board announced in the newspaper that it was giving an across-the-board $300 raise to all teachers to compensate for the rise in the cost of living. Of course, this necessitated a local increase in school taxes. A citizen group organized and requested that the local board and superintendent grant it time at the board's next meeting to discuss merit rating as a part of the new salary schedule. The request was granted, and over 100 people came to the open meeting, all of them with strong feelings in favor of the merit salary schedule.

The merit salary schedule was developed by the superintendent and several principals, but because of the pressure of time and other reasons, the teachers were not consulted. The following year the schedule was placed in operation. Some teachers complained bitterly, and a few resigned to take employment elsewhere; others thought it was a good idea to reward the competent.

After three years of operation, the teachers, the administrators, the school board, and the community were all unhappy with the merit salary schedule. The criteria for evaluation had proved to be inadequate. The evaluators were not trained well enough, or they did not have ample time to do their work well. Parents objected when their children were assigned to teachers who held low ratings rather than high ratings. The merit rating system made it difficult to employ needed personnel. The teachers themselves came to believe that the merit salary schedule imposed upon them would not work, since they had no part in its planning. The board of education was forced to replace the merit salary schedule with a single salary schedule.

Case Number Two—Brassville

Brassville school system, in a suburban area, had ample funds to begin a merit salary schedule. Its personnel office had a long list of applicants with excellent qualifications who were waiting for the opportunity to be employed by the Brassville school board. The maximum wage provided by the salary schedule was more than $7,000. The superintendent, after consultation with administrators and teachers, submitted a plan to the board of education which included teacher competency along with experience and training as determiners of salary. The board accepted the suggestion and asked that the minimum salary be more than $3,000 and the maximum be more than $8,000.

The superintendent reported the board's action to the faculty, who accepted the idea. A committee was appointed to develop the criteria for evaluation. Also assigned to this committee was the task of making recommendations concerning procedures for carrying out the merit salary plan. The committee developed criteria and plans of action which were submitted to the faculty for criticisms and suggestions. It was agreed that the principals would do the evaluating, with the faculty deciding methods and procedures. This merit salary schedule is still in operation after five years. There have been no serious complaints from parents; however, each year the faculty reviews its decision to keep or reject the plan.

To What Extent Are In-Service Educational Programs Effective?

In-service education is intended to help school personnel grow in professionalism and competency, and it involves the efforts of administrative and supervisory officials as well as of the teachers. It is generally agreed that all teachers need some type of in-service education. There is continuous demand for teachers to learn new methodology and content and to gain better insights into human behavior. It is doubtful if any educator, regardless of the degrees he holds, is in such an advanced state of professional development that he could not profit by in-service education. The issue is not the need for in-service education; it is the question of how good our in-service educational programs are. There are more than 100 activities designed to help with in-service education. Unfortunately, there is room for considerable doubt as to the success of many such programs.

If an in-service educational program is to be successful, it must have as one of its major purposes to help teachers improve their professional competence. In order for a program to meet this need, it must begin with the basic needs of teachers. Far too many in-service educational programs begin with what the administrators think are teacher needs. Administrative problems may be the same as teacher problems in some instances, but, for the greater part, it is wise to consider what teachers have to offer and to use their strengths rather than to pinpoint several weaknesses and attempt to make them over.

Evaluation of teacher improvement must be sound and fair. Some school systems use teacher reactions, others use affirmations of individuals, and still others use mere observation. Group evaluation and self-evaluation are two additional types of appraisal frequently used.

Many teachers object to being rated individually. They assume that any type of rating other than observation and self-evaluation, both highly subjective, represents direct criticism and is dangerous to morale. There is good evidence, however, that this is not always the case.[2] Morale is related to a vast number of variables rather than to one isolated factor.

Administrators have not always understood their role in

___

[2] See B. J. Chandler, "Salary Policies and Teacher Morale," *Educational Administration and Supervision,* **45:**107–110, March, 1959.

providing leadership for in-service education. Next to the nomination of personnel for the school system and working with the board of education, perhaps the greatest single task expected of a superintendent or principal is to help the faculty members he has selected to grow and to develop within the profession. It is not enough to establish workshops, to plan in-service meetings, and to encourage teachers to secure advanced degrees. There should be a plan for evaluation of the results of the in-service techniques other than self-evaluation.

In-service educational programs that require compulsory attendance and do not permit the teachers to take part in the planning of the activity have had a negative effect upon evaluation. Although it is highly desirable to have wide participation in in-service programs, it is doubtful if compulsory participation is fruitful. If leadership is vigorous, it is likely that most employees will choose to take part in a program designed for their growth. If participants cannot be led to see value in the program, there is little hope for their gaining much from forced attendance.

When teachers are aware of the reason for in-service education, they tend to enjoy the program more and to contribute more to it. The main factor to be concerned with in promoting an in-service program is securing the interest and enthusiasm of the teachers for the study of problems with which they are concerned. Teacher participation in the program does not result after the formation of the program; rather, the in-service program should reflect teacher interest in the further study of their own immediate problems and should be planned to facilitate that purpose. If there is sufficient interest on the part of the faculty for the program, then the in-service program may be introduced. Learning usually takes place best when it begins with matters of real interest and concern to the learner.

Evaluation of in-service educational programs is improving, although definitive procedures have not been developed. Early evaluation in this field consisted largely of studies of the attitudes of teachers toward supervision and administrators. More recently, the reactions of teachers to various in-service devices have indicated that shared experiences such as policy shaping, planning and conducting faculty meetings, and cooperative problem solving are the most effective.

Case Number Three illustrates the type of reaction one may find when in-service educational programs have required attendance and when school employees have no part in planning the program. Case Number Four illustrates an in-service program based upon cooperative action.

Case Number Three—Ducktown

The school district of Ducktown initiated a self-study program for several schools during one year. The program was sponsored jointly by a university and the Ducktown school system. One of the senior high schools was told it had been selected to go through a self-evaluation. Attendance was required on the part of all teachers for this program. Teachers who desired credit could register with the local university and receive graduate or undergraduate credit applicable toward a degree program. All teachers met for the same length of time, although some were not taking the training for credit. The time spent at meetings amounted to more than thirty hours during the year, and additional time was required to make preparation for the meetings, which were biweekly. Consultant help was available from the local university and from the central office of the administration. The principal was not very enthusiastic about the program.

At the end of the school year the more than 100 teachers

were asked to respond to a self-evaluation questionnaire. The instrument also sought the reaction of participants to the success of the program. In general, the teachers were very critical. They expressed concern over not being consulted prior to inauguration of the self-study and over not having been given a choice of various activities in which they might have taken part. General resentment and discontent were expressed. The teachers also objected to having to attend meetings at the end of the school day when they were tired; they felt that in-service programs should be financed by the local board of education so that time could be set aside during the school day for this work. Compulsory attendance got its share of criticism too.

Case Number Four—White Hill

White Hill school system is fortunate in that it has an abundance of wealth and taxable resources. Its salaries are among the highest in its state. The school district has enjoyed dynamic leadership from the superintendent and the board of education for many years. The administrators, supervisors, and teachers are among the best in the country.

A few years ago this school system developed a summer workshop for its personnel that is somewhat unique. More than 700 employees of the system were invited to participate. Teachers and administrators studied intensively their own professional problems and practices and weighed them against sound educational theory and research. Each teacher concerned himself with questions which he helped formulate in study groups of his own choice prior to the workshop, which lasted a week.

The workshop included all teaching and administrative personnel. It cut across all grade and departmental lines, and each person was paid his regular contractual rate for work. Consultants were employed from six leading universities for the areas, chosen by the teachers, for study. Although attendance was voluntary, more than 98 per cent of the employees elected to participate. Reactions from teachers and administrators indicate that they rate the program, which is now in its seventh year, very highly.

3 7 1 . 2
J o n

Are the Effects of Tenure for Teachers Desirable?

The term "tenure," as used here, refers to the kind of school employment in which a teacher, having served as probationary period of so many years, has his job security protected by law or school-board policy and cannot be dismissed except through certain legally specified procedures. No effort is made to distinguish between continuing contracts and tenure.

The principal purpose of tenure laws is to provide job security during good behavior and prevent arbitrary demotions and dismissals, and to improve the teaching profession by keeping the competent personnel employed. The National Education Association and the various state associations have been active in promoting teacher-tenure laws and policies. A majority of states today have some provisions for tenure, New Jersey and Wisconsin being among the first to provide tenure laws.

Although tenure laws are becoming more widespread, there is a variance of opinion concerning the arguments for and against tenure for teachers. These arguments concerning tenure have been debated by a number of outstanding authorities.[3]

[3] See Raleigh W. Holmstedt, *A Study of the Effects of Teacher Tenure Laws in New Jersey,* doctor's dissertation, Columbia University, New York, 1932; Chandler and Petty, *op. cit.,* pp. 352–355; Elsbree and Reutter, *op. cit.,* pp. 201–207; and National Education Association, Committee on Tenure and Academic Freedom, *Teacher Tenure Manual,* The Association, Washington, D.C., 1950.

Among the reasons advanced for tenure are:

1. Teacher tenure is a basic principle of economic efficiency.

2. Tenure helps to protect the teacher from unwarranted political attacks.

3. The teacher is freed from anxiety of being dismissed without just cause.

4. Tenure helps to secure better teachers because it encourages a more careful selection of faculty.

5. There is little evidence that tenure reduces interest in professional development.

6. Tenure reduces the temptation for teachers to violate professional ethics and to yield to the whims of pressure groups.

In opposition to tenure, one may find the following arguments:

1. Incompetent and undesirable teachers may be retained in the profession, since tenure makes it more difficult to dismiss them.

2. It may become more difficult to supervise some teachers who know they have security of position.

3. Contrary to much popular opinion, tenure has, in a number of instances, increased teacher turnover.

4. Tenure of office is not protected by law in other professions.

5. The public has, in many instances, questioned the practice of permitting teachers to hold their positions despite their failure to do a competent job.

6. Good teachers do not need to be protected by tenure legislation.

Case Number Five illustrates how tenure laws enabled a competent teacher to get redress for being dismissed without a proper hearing. Case Number Six illustrates how an incompetent teacher was retained in the teaching profession because tenure made it more difficult to remove her.

Case Number Five—Mr. Baker

Mr. Baker was in his middle thirties and had taught social studies in high school for eight years. He was well liked and respected by faculty members, students, and the community. Upon completion of his master's degree, he accepted an appointment in a much larger high school in an adjoining city system. The first two years found him happy and doing well in his new position. His third year in the new position was under a new superintendent. Mr. Baker did not campaign for or against the newly elected superintendent.

It was a law in this particular state that teachers were to be notified by April 1 if they were not yet on tenure and were not to be employed for the following year. Mr. Baker did not receive any communication from the superintendent or board of education. The last week of the school year, the local newspaper carried a list of the new teachers and old teachers who would be employed at the high school the following year. Mr. Baker was told by a fellow teacher that his name was not on the list. After checking the newspaper, Mr. Baker asked his principal about this. The principal suggested that Mr. Baker talk with the superintendent. He did, and found that he had not been given permanent tenure. Mr. Baker consulted the state teachers' association, which furnished legal aid for him to fight the case. By the time the case came to court, Mr. Baker had been employed by another board of education nearby, and the school term was in its third month of operation. The court ruled that Mr. Baker should have been notified in writing prior to or by April 1 if he were not to be employed the following year or given tenure. The court ordered the

board of education to pay Mr. Baker's salary for one year at
the previous rate, although he was now teaching in another
district.

Case Number Six—Miss Jones

Miss Jones was a teacher of home economics in a large
consolidated high school. She held both the bachelor's and
master's degrees from the local state university and was starting
her fifth year of teaching in this particular school. Miss Jones
had done outstanding work at the university and in her practice
teaching. Her teaching record was one that would make any
teacher very proud.

In October of the fifth year of her teaching at the consolidated high school, her behavior became unusual. Miss Jones
was single and roomed with two other unmarried teachers.
She told her principal that the other two teachers were stealing
her undergarments and hosiery. She complained that the students were continuously stealing her grade book and other
personal belongings. She also felt that her landlord was taking
her jewelry and personal effects. She complained of ill health
and was unable to keep her classes from disturbing other
classes.

Several conferences with the principal seemed to have no
desirable effect. Children were laughing at her in the halls and
classrooms. The principal suggested that she have a medical
examination, but she refused. Later, the superintendent and
the board of education were told of the situation. Miss Jones
was invited to meet with the principal and superintendent, but
she failed to appear. In a desperate effort to do something for
the children in home economics, the superintendent asked her
to resign, but she refused. Since she had permanent tenure,
the board of education did not wish to initiate a court case that

would involve them as well as the unfortunate teacher, who, apparently, was well liked by the community. Two months later, Miss Jones became physically ill and had to be replaced by a substitute teacher, at which time she finally did resign.

Should the Faculty Participate in Policy Development?

Leadership has a variety of meanings. For example, the military service bases its idea of leadership on a functional approach that is highly disciplined and authoritarian. In the business world the idea of leadership is influenced greatly by the profit motive. Our public schools have a different function to serve in our society. Our schools must be workshops of democracy. Educational leadership implies ability and readiness to inspire, guide, and help others. The democratic leader is interested in bringing people together in order that they may work effectively and happily to achieve agreed-upon purposes. Group organization cannot be forced upon a collection of individuals; it must grow out of relationships of the people who compose it.

Somewhere between autocratic and laissez-faire types of leadership lies the concept of true democratic leadership. The leader of such an organization must be a real member of the group; he must share the same desires and seek the same goals as do the other members. Although he is the leader, he must remember that authority resides with every other member of the group as that member becomes capable of using it for the promotion and enhancement of the group, and that it may be delegated as the occasion demands.

No administrator's method of operation is so good as to do away with all stress and friction, but the administrator who seeks the advice and help of the staff and community, who knows when to delegate responsibility, who makes decisions based on group thinking, who uses discussion and reason, as opposed to pressure, force, and ultimatums, has the best chance to make democratic administration work.

An administrator must do more than secure opinions of associates; he must evaluate their ideas and give them an opportunity to work. Teachers, on the other hand, must also be willing to accept the responsibility that is entailed in their participation. Neither administrators nor teachers have anything to lose in sharing responsibility, and both have much to gain.

The following arguments are sometimes presented against teacher participation in policy development:

1. Many faculty members do not understand the nature of administrative problems.

2. A large number of faculty members are not trained in the democratic process and are not qualified to participate.

3. There are many faculty members who prefer to leave the administration of schools to those who are trained for it.

4. Teachers should be assigned to study only minor educational problems if they are to have any part at all in policy development.

5. The power to develop policies should be vested in one person—the head administrator.

6. Superintendents who invite teacher participation lose leadership status.

7. Teacher participation in administration is a time-consuming factor and creates additional work for the overburdened administrator.

In favor of teacher participation in policy development, one may find the following arguments:

1. No administrator, regardless of training and experience, has all the answers in regard to administration.

2. Teachers should have a part in planning the policies that will affect their welfare.

3. Teachers are more likely to accept and to help execute policies which they have assisted in developing.

4. To the extent that they are willing and able, teachers should have the right and the opportunity to contribute ideas to the administrator.

5. Teacher morale, efficiency, and support of a school system by the school personnel will be increased by participation in formulating and executing the policies of the educational system.

6. If teachers are encouraged to participate in policy making, it is much more likely that they will know and understand the activities for which they are responsible.

A good administrator will make it possible for teachers to discuss and participate in policy making where needed. Long discussions and consultations take much valuable time but, in the long run, will save time because of increased understandings and efficiency. Good teacher morale is a prerequisite to a good instructional program. There is a direct relationship between high morale and human efficiency. An environment conducive to strong morale is not likely to be achieved by chance. Administrators should recognize its importance and accept a major responsibility for advancing it.

Case Number Seven illustrates what can happen when a large proportion of the faculty members are not trained in the democratic process of policy making. Case Number Eight gives an example of an administrator who realized that he needed the help of the faculty and did everything possible to encourage teachers to share their ideas with him and with each other.

Case Number Seven—Mr. Slatts

Mr. Slatts has served as a principal of a large high school for several years and had enjoyed a high degree of success in his leadership role. As a result of his excellent leadership, he was appointed superintendent of a city system. Upon his arrival at the new position, he assumed that the faculties of this school system could operate in the cooperative, friendly way that his former faculty had done. He had them elect one teacher from each school, both elementary and secondary, to serve with each principal as a part of his advisory council. Many of the teachers thought this was silly. They thought Mr. Slatts was the boss, and as such, he should make most decisions. This council held meetings every two weeks. Mr. Slatts used this group to try out new ideas and suggestions and to secure teacher reaction to changes. This committee was rather large, and many of the teachers said little. Some of the elected representatives laughed at the very idea of their being on the council. Mr. Slatts tried to get the teachers' ideas about existing policies and procedures. He questioned, for example, the purpose behind the rule that teachers had to sign in and out at each individual school, and he wanted to know why all children had to march in straight lines to the lunchroom. Mr. Slatts asked the committee to study such questions and report their findings.

All that Mr. Slatts ever learned from the council was that its members were satisfied with things as they were and that, in any case, he was boss and should make all necessary decisions. If he demanded changes in procedures, they would be made, but the teachers did not feel it was their job to make policy.

Case Number Eight—Mr. Bonner

Mr. Bonner had been superintendent of this large city school system for more than ten years. He had always encouraged his faculties to make suggestions, through their principals, to his office when needed changes or new ideas were discovered. For the past five years the school district had held a week of preplanning before schools opened and a week of postplanning at the end of the school year, but there were some complaints that nothing ever really happened during the planning sessions except that announcements were made and "gripes" aired. Mr. Bonner and the principals and supervisors decided that it would be wise to develop a questionnaire and ask each faculty member to fill it out anonymously. The instrument was constructed to find out what district-wide problems the teachers would like to discuss during the planning sessions. Almost 100 per cent of the faculty returned the questionnaire completely filled out. Many made written suggestions in addition. The problems identified for study included: "Do all schools have to teach the same thing at the same time?" "How can communication between the elementary and high schools be improved?" "Can ways be provided to enable teachers to participate more during the planning sessions rather than just be talked to by outside consultants?" "Can the activities planned and carried out during the planning sessions be mimeographed for distribution to all schools within the district?" "Would it be possible for two or more faculties to spend two days of the planning session together?"

Mr. Bonner and the members of the administrative group accepted the suggestions, and plans were made to discuss city-wide policies for half of the preplanning session and for two days of the postplanning session. A subsequent evaluation sheet indicated that more than 95 per cent of the participants were very satisfied with the new organization of the planning sessions.

Questions for Discussion

Case Number One

1. Why did the merit salary schedule fail?
2. How would you have gone about initiating a merit salary schedule in this situation?

Case Number Two

3. To what do you attribute the success of the merit salary schedule in this case?
4. Would a merit salary schedule work in your school system? Why?

Case Number Three

5. Should in-service educational programs have compulsory attendance? Why?
6. Assuming that you were the administrator in this case, what would you do differently?

Case Number Four

7. What are the factors which contributed to the success of in-service education in this case?
8. Are teachers capable of identifying their problems to the extent that in-service education can be based upon this approach? Why?

Case Number Five

9. Is tenure necessary to protect competent teachers? Why?
10. On what grounds did Mr. Baker win his case?

Case Number Six

11. Had you been the administrator involved, would you have dismissed Miss Jones? If so, on what grounds?

12. Do you see any reason why Miss Jones should have been kept as a faculty member? How could this case have been handled differently?

Case Number Seven

13. What was wrong with Mr. Slatts' approach to the democratic process in planning?

14. How would you have handled this case if you had been the administrator?

Case Number Eight

15. Identify some of the elements of planning which Mr. Bonner used that you think are good. Why?

16. How would you have handled this case had you been Mr. Bonner? Discuss other ways it could have been treated successfully.

Selected Readings

American Association of School Administrators, *The American School Superintendency,* Thirtieth Yearbook, The Association, Washington, D.C., 1952, Chap. VII.

Ayars, Albert L., *Administering the People's Schools,* McGraw-Hill Book Company, Inc., New York, 1957, Chap. 7.

Chandler, B. J., and Petty, Paul V., *Personnel Management in School Administration,* World Book Company, Yonkers, N.Y., 1955, Chaps. 3, 12.

Elsbree, Willard, and Reutter, Edmund, Jr., *Staff Personnel in the Public Schools,* Prentice-Hall, Inc., Englewood Cliffs, N.J., 1954, Chaps. 6, 8.

Holmstedt, Raleigh W., *A Study of the Effects of Teacher Tenure Laws in New Jersey,* doctor's dissertation, Columbia University, New York, 1932.

Jones, James J., "Teacher Morale and Administration," *The Clearing House,* 34: 291–292, January, 1958.

McCall, William A., *Measurement of Teacher Merit,* Publication No. 284, State Superintendent of Public Instruction, Raleigh, N.C., 1952.

National Education Association, Research Division, *Reference on Teacher Rating and Evaluation,* November, 1955 (mimeographed) 11 pp.; Committee on Tenure and Academic Freedom, *Teacher Tenure Manual,* The Association, Washington, D.C., 1950.

National School Boards Association, Inc., *Seven Studies,* The Association, Chicago, 1958, pp. 42–45.

ISSUES DEALING WITH CURRICULUM

6.

PROBABLY the two most important sets of issues affecting the basic progress of education are those taken up in this and the next chapter; namely, issues dealing directly with curriculum and with instruction. Actually, all other issues also, at least indirectly, involve the learning processes of children, but the child is directly affected by problems of curriculum and instruction.

What should be taught in our schools is an ever-present issue. It probably has no permanent solution, since changing times would seem to necessitate an ever-changing curriculum. Times of social stress may dictate an emphasis on a social curriculum, rapid technological change may dictate emphasis on the sciences, and economic stress may result in an even different emphasis. A child may be trained in one emphasis, only to discover that, during his later productive years, another need is predominant. It is a dilemma that has always confronted those who determine what shall be taught. There is increasing evidence that there cannot be any one permanent solution to the problem; and, consequently, more and more professionals and laymen are coming to believe that a curriculum that educates for change may be the best approach.

The areas of controversy discussed below include the scope of the educational program, the determiners of the curriculum, self-contained classrooms in the elementary school, and the comprehensive nature of the secondary school. The way schools handle such problems will be reflected in their public-relations programs.

What Should Be the Scope of the Educational Program?

This issue is one of long standing. It may involve what people often class as frills, the purposes of education, crash programs, immediate and long-range demands, common core of knowledge, and the community feeling toward education. Some people feel that the schools are undertaking too much, that they would do well to limit themselves to the things they are best equipped to teach; others feel that the school should be responsible for doing many things which, although they may previously have been done by the home, are now best performed by the school.

The following questions come to mind when one begins to discuss this issue. What subjects are to be classed as "frill" courses? Music, for example, is a frill to some and a very solid subject to others. Should the high school be mainly college preparatory, more or less ignoring those thousands who have neither the desire, the opportunity, nor the aptitude to attend college? Is there a place for safety and driver-training courses in the high-school curriculum? If not, how can the growing rate of traffic accidents be checked? Do schools have an obligation to help in character building of youth? Is it advisable to guide students only at certain periods and ignore them at other times?

People may be swayed by immediate and sometimes temporary needs and recommend a crash program to meet them, only to discover, in a few years, that the need is no longer pressing and that another and perhaps opposite need is clamoring for attention. It must be kept in mind, however, that immediate and perhaps temporary demands cannot always be ignored. Fortunately, there is evidence which indicates that a common core of knowledge and training is necessary so that all children of all ages will develop into responsible citizens, no matter what particular emphasis is called for by currently pressing societal needs. It is generally agreed that all children need to know about and understand the problems of our physical universe, and that subjects dealing with the physical world are essential. For one to live happily and profitably in any age, the development of a sense of values and a sense of responsibility is essential. Thus, courses in the humanities, art, music, and philosophy cannot be left out of the educational program. Last, but certainly not least, is the necessity for knowledge and understanding of one's social institutions. This makes it necessary for a student to study the social and behavorial sciences. Neglect of any of these areas deprives a child of his just heritage. This is not to say there can or should be a universal type of program. Individual schools will need to adjust to their specific needs, but this basic core serves as a good point of departure.

Case Number One illustrates how a local school system refused to add needed courses because it wished to avoid what is called "frill" courses. In Case Number Two a "crash program" resulted in an overemphasis upon mathematics and science in the curriculum, and in this case much of the planning ignored the individual needs of pupils.

Case Number One—Steeltown

The community of Steeltown is adjacent to one of our large American cities. Its people work in steel mills and at other laboring jobs, with few of the inhabitants belonging to the professions. Although most of the children come from homes of the laboring classes, the average income per family is equal to, or in some instances greater than, the national average. Despite the relatively good economic standing, living conditions within the school district leave much to be desired.

Steeltown school district is a consolidated one which has a community school that houses grades one through twelve. The total pupil enrollment approximates 900. Its organization is the 6-6 plan, that is, six grades in elementary and six in high school.

Although the state recommended that music be offered in each school district, it had not enforced this suggestion. An interested group of parents approached the school principal and requested that music be added to the curriculum the following year. They gave many excellent arguments for the importance of music in our daily lives. It was suggested that a special music teacher be employed to teach once a week in each grade within the elementary school. Also it was suggested that two courses in music be offered as electives in high school, and that a part-time music teacher be appointed for this purpose.

The principal invited this group of parents, perhaps twenty in number, to meet with the faculty and explain its proposal. The faculty accepted the idea wholeheartedly and suggested that the proposal be submitted to the superintendent and board of education at their next meeting.

The principal requested two parents from the group and

two teachers to accompany him to the meeting with the super-intendent and the board. The principal, teachers, and parents made the presentation to the board of education. Three members of the five-man board scoffed at the idea of employing special teachers to teach music to the children of steelworkers. One member said, "It is unreasonable to assume that children from this school district have a need for music that goes beyond what a regular classroom teacher can give. I never had special-ized instruction in music, and I have done all right." Another board member said, "Music is a frill and should not be paid for by public funds. If parents want their children taught music, let them pay for it on a private basis."

The final count found three member in opposition to the idea, one member in favor, and another member undecided. The net result was refusal by the board to consider employment of additional music teachers for the district. The superin-tendent was sympathetic to the suggested music program and tried to encourage the board to see its benefits, but his efforts were futile.

Case Number Two—Central High School

Soon after the Russians placed a satellite in orbit, the parents of children in Central High School began to talk among them-selves concerning the lack of science training at the school. Agitated by the accounts in newspapers and magazines of our nation's scientific failures, a group of parents from the local school went to see the principal. They wanted four courses required in mathematics and four courses in science. They also suggested more homework and a more rigorous type of instruction for all pupils.

The local principal attempted to tell the parents of the many difficulties involved in such changes. First, he pointed out that more than half of the pupils attending Central High School could not pass more than the two years of mathematics and two years of science now being required for graduation. He wanted to know what would happen to those who could not pass more rigorous work. One parent, speaking for a small but vocal group, said, "We are not worried about the masses, we want our children to learn if they are capable; if not, they should be sent home so the other pupils who have the ability to pursue difficult work can get what is coming to them." Another parent said, "Too many pupils are being allowed to graduate from Central today. When I was a high-school student here, only the best students were expected to graduate."

This group of parents began meeting weekly to discuss their personal views on what should be done about the curriculum. Finally, they met with the parent-teacher association, whose members receive with mixed reactions the idea of increasing mathematics to four years and science to four years. Again, the principal and some members of the local faculty raised questions concerning the advisability of the change or, at least, of making this a requirement rather than putting it on an elective basis.

But pressure mounted until the faculty at Central High School finally agreed that a "crash program" in science and mathematics would be begun. At the end of the first year of the program, several pupils were not promoted because of inability to do the additional work required in mathematics or science, among whom were some whose parents had insisted on the "get-tough" program.

Another parental group formed in opposition to the first group and requested that the local school return to its former program. One parent said, "We self-appointed authorities in curriculum and instruction lack much of the knowledge that is

necessary to decide what should be taught at Central High."
A second parent reported, "The board employs teachers to
work with the state and local authorities to help decide what
our youth should study. I can see no reason for our interfering." After that one-year trial, the "crash program" was
stopped.

Who Should Be the Determiners of the Curriculum?

Recommended responsibility for this task varies from the
school administrator, on the one extreme, to society as a
whole, on the other. Some of the confusion stems from lack
of understanding, by both parents and teachers, of the term
"curriculum." Some understand it to mean the "course of
study"; others consider it to mean "all the experiences that
children have in school." Where such confusion exists, the
first step is to agree on a workable definition that will serve
as a basis for discussion.

Curriculum-planning responsibilities vary in practice as
well as in theory; therefore, it is important, in discussing this
problem, to recognize some agencies that indirectly help decide
what shall be the curriculum. In many of our smaller schools,
the requirements developed by various personnel for regional
and state accreditation agencies, which schools must fulfill to
be fully accredited, often become the blueprint for the curriculum. Schoolmen are also pressured by local citizens to
offer the necessary courses and experiences to meet the college
admission requirements which are established by college and
university faculties.

Within every community there are citizens with attitudes of
some type toward public education. They may favor strong
public schools, or they may be somewhat neutral or strongly
opposed to public schools. This attitude may stem from the

cultural values held by the local people and, to some degree, from traditions which have become established. The school system must function within the framework or pattern of values, traditions, attitudes, and concepts of the people. This means that there are views and beliefs which are commonly accepted by our society, and the school is expected to employ personnel who will carry out these ideas. In order to break away from tradition, it may be necessary to fight many battles and to struggle to introduce change. This requires a great deal of initiative and informed leadership.

Involved in decisions about curriculum work will necessarily be the legal mandates or sanctions of the various states. Included in this group will be the state department of education and its personnel. Rules and regulations of the state board of education must be carried out. Most of these rules are concerned with minimum essentials and broad, general plans which are usually meant to set the guidelines for district planning. Within the broad areas defined by the state level should be personnel connected with local school district and individual faculties of various schools. Principals, administrators, supervisors, and others may work with teachers in either a district or a school setting to plan curriculum. School-board members and lay persons from the local communities may be invited to participate, and, in some schools, pupils have served as a part of curriculum committees.

The individuals and groups discussed above have varying degrees of responsibility for determining what should be included in the curriculum under the present organization of public schools. Using pupil needs and the demands of our society as a base, both professionals and lay citizens are responsible for developing a curriculum in a cooperative manner, with the professionals providing the leadership and technical advice and the lay citizens helping wherever they have contributions to make.

Case Number Three illustrates the difficulties faced by a small school in meeting demands for curriculum changes. In Case Number Four we see the curriculum determined by individuals and groups working cooperatively.

Case Number Three—Noble High School

Noble High School is located in a rural area and is in its third year of operation as a consolidated school. Previously, its students attended six other small elementary and high schools. The total enrollment in grades nine to twelve is only 300. The program for high-school students is based largely upon what the state suggested for graduation requirements and the courses necessary to get its graduates admitted to college.

The principal had a curriculum-planning committee composed of both lay and professional members. The committee suggested that courses in driver education, business education, and advanced shopwork be added to the curriculum. A questionnaire was developed by the curriculum committee and submitted to every fifth parent. Returns indicated that they desired the addition of these courses, but many stated that they wanted most of all to have courses offered that would enable their boys and girls to be eligible for college.

When the curriculum committee presented its findings to the principal and he, in turn, submitted their findings to the board of education, several questions came up for discussion. The board of education and the superintendent were very much in favor of adding the suggested courses but were unable to see how they could be financed, as additional teaching personnel would be required. They did not feel that any present offerings should be discontinued. All the board could do was to encourage the local school to be patient and to suggest that the committee work for a higher tax rate the following year in order to pay for the school curriculum which they desired.

Although Noble School has not secured the additional courses it desired, the last report indicates that the board of education, the local citizen groups, and the professional personnel are all working diligently toward such future plans.

Case Number Four—Price Elementary School

Price School enrolled approximately 500 pupils in grades one through eight. Located in a small village, Price School had the advantage of being near the center of the school population. The citizens of the community felt very close to the school. They visited often and attended most of the school activities that were open to the public. Although Price School was only two years old and many citizens had not lived in the community even for that length of time, there was a feeling that the school was making every effort to meet the needs of its pupils.

Part of the public confidence in the school was the result of the existence of an active citizen committee. A large block of this committee recommended that conversational Spanish be offered in all the elementary grades. At first, this consideration was met with resistance by the faculty, but, after several weeks of study by the school personnel and the administrators, it was agreed to try the adventure on an experimental basis for one year. Staffing this experience was not difficult; the regular teachers received teaching assistance from Spanish-speaking citizens who were paid by the county board of education. Parents were assured that their children would not be expected to become experts in Spanish and that no part of what they termed "the fundamentals" of elementary education would be slighted because of this addition to the curriculum.

At the end of the first year, an evaluation by teachers, pupils, and parents indicated that the new course had been worth very little, and the school discontinued it. In the meantime, however, local citizens had been made to feel that they had a legitimate role to play as advisers in curriculum planning.

Should There Be Self-Contained Classrooms in the Elementary School?

Should we teach arithmetic, or should we teach Mary, or should we teach Mary arithmetic? Some people believe that the self-contained classroom puts the major emphasis on knowing the child and neglects the subject matter; others feel that departmentalized organizations, in placing the major emphasis on subject, neglects the child himself. Actually, what is desired by most laymen and professionals is a good balance between the two, with neither side neglected.

Proponents of the self-contained classroom believe that this organization gives teachers a better chance to know their students—their background, their home life, their weaknesses and strengths. They feel that this arrangement enables the teacher to serve as a counselor as well as a teacher, doing away with the necessity for counselors except those specially trained to deal with exceptional cases. They also believe that a teacher, under this organization, has a much better chance to help the child correlate subject matter.

Proponents of departmentalization in the elementary school maintain that this organization lends itself to better teaching of subject matter. Teachers in this kind of a system will be better trained in the subjects they handle and will thus be better able to detect children gifted in the teachers' areas of specialization and to offer more expert guidance in these areas. Advocates of this organization believe that it offers better opportunities for screening and placement of students in classes and that it militates against neglecting either the fast, in-between, or slow learner. They also claim that specialized school equipment costs less when it can be located in one room for one teacher, as opposed to spreading it around for every teacher.

To the parents and citizens these arguments become very confusing. They ask, if the school is operated under one type of organization, must their children suffer from loss of the advantages claimed under the other system. Many feel or are led to feel that they, the parents, have to accept one and are not too happy about it. These opinions do not make for good relations between the school and community and should be avoided whenever possible.

Facts show that school systems vary widely in practice, and it is impossible to get agreement except in the many schools which utilize the best of each kind of organization. It is erroneous to think that teachers who are well trained in institutions of higher learning continuously neglect either side of the argument.

Parents need to be told and reassured that, under either organization, their children need not be segmented, but that they remain unique individuals, and that no part of their development will be neglected. It is probable, however, that during a child's early years in school more careful attention will be paid to his social training than will be the case in his later years. It has not been by chance that children in the elementary grades have been placed in self-contained classrooms, which are generally considered to foster such attention.

Case Number Five depicts the advantage of continuity of learning experiences when an elementary school is organized on a self-contained classroom basis. Case Number Six indicates some of the dangers of departmentalization in the elementary school.

Case Number Five—Deep Run Elementary School

Deep Run Elementary School is in an isolated community which has a total population of around 5,000 people. Its people are proud of the school's achievements and the progress made by its pupils. Its classroom organization is self-contained, without any specialized instructors from the central or district office. Each teacher has a grade and teaches all the subjects felt necessary at this level of operation. Although most grades number twenty-five to thirty-five pupils, the strengths and weaknesses and over-all achievements of each student are known to his teacher. Subjects can be correlated in many instances, and large blocks of subject matter may be attacked for concentrated study over a period of days.

Recently, Deep Run School gave standardized tests of mental ability and achievement from grade two through grade six. Pupils were compared with other schools within the school district that had the departmentalized organization, and their subject-matter achievement in general was equal to or above average for the district. It is felt by the teachers that the attitudes and study habits developed in this school are worthy of high praise and consideration.

This school has had its program of self-contained classrooms for six years, prior to that time having been organized on a departmentalized basis. A survey of the faculty found 95 per cent in favor of continuing the self-contained classroom approach, and parents are also favorable to the program.

Case Number Six—Palm Elementary School

For ten years Palm Elementary School had operated on a self-contained classroom basis, but numerous complaints from parents and other interested citizens brought about a two-year tryout of teaching on a departmentalized basis.

Effort was made to place teachers in their areas of interest and training, and extra funds were spent for room equipment for special subjects. New faculty members were selected on the basis of their special training and how well they fitted into the new organization.

Achievement tests were administered at the beginning and end of the year in each subject field. These results were compared with those obtained under the previous organization, but no achievement increase of any significance was noted. It was true that some of the very best students seemed to achieve more in certain subjects than formerly, but the over-all improvement was not as much as in the years past, although the student mental-ability mean score was five points higher.

A survey of the faculty indicated that more than 65 per cent felt that the disadvantages of departmentalization outweighed its advantages. In addition, parents expressed displeasure at the lack of knowledge teachers had concerning individual pupils.

Should the Secondary School Be Comprehensive in Nature?

The question of the relative merits of the comprehensive high school and the specialized one is an issue that is likely to be prominent in the educational picture for years to come. In any case, it is much easier to recognize the advisability of consolidation than it is to accomplish it. Schools serve the community in other ways than by an educational program and may be so inextricably woven into the fabric of a community that more would be destroyed than gained by any attempt to abolish a specialized school in the interest of consolidation.

The comprehensive high school in America is usually thought of as a four-year school that offers programs which include college-preparatory, general-education, and vocational curriculums. Perhaps one of the strongest advocates of the comprehensive high school is James B. Conant, who has devoted much time and study to the American high schools. In his book, *Education and Liberty,* he speaks fervently in favor of the comprehensive high school.

> I suggest that we adhere to the principle of a comprehensive high school with a common core of studies and differentiated special programs, but in so doing make more effort to identify the gifted youth and give him or her more rigorous academic training in languages and mathematics. . . .
>
> Today in the larger cities of the United States the separation of students into different schools depending on their academic ability and their vocational ambitions is common practice. I have become increasingly convinced that such an arrangement is a mistake, for it fails to provide a basis for growth of mutual understanding between different cultural, religious, and occupational groups. The primary schools by and large do provide this opportunity; so do the high schools in the towns and smaller cities.[1]

Other points in favor of the comprehensive high school include the following:

1. It provides more variability of program and meets the needs of more individuals than does a specialized high school.

2. Many areas of the United States do not have ample

---

[1] James B. Conant, *Education and Liberty,* Harvard University Press, Cambridge, Mass., 1953, pp. 57-61.

student population for a specialized high school but do have enough pupils for a comprehensive high school.

3. Specialized high schools often screen applicants very carefully, and the pupils who are rejected are forced to attend another school, irrespective of inconvenience.

4. Operation of vocational schools tends to cost more per pupil than does similar training given in a comprehensive high school.

5. General education is neglected in specialized and vocational schools.

Specialized high schools, frequently called vocational, trade, or technical high schools, are generally thought of as schools which emphasize vocational curriculums. The major purpose of these schools is not general education but vocational preparation.

Although comprehensive high schools may be inevitable where there is only one school in a community, a strong case can be made for specialized high schools in the larger communities, where economic demands and individual group needs make vocational and technical training imperative.

The major arguments against the comprehensive high school may be summarized as follows:

1. It reduces the depth of individual study for all pupils.

2. If there is more than one comprehensive high school in the system, facilities and equipment may be duplicated.

3. It is easier to motivate students who are enrolled in a specialized school and who have many factors in common.

From a good public-relations point of view, the citizens of a community should be apprised of both sides of the vocational versus comprehensive issue before they are asked to approve the direction a community should take. This implies citizen participation in planning the school curriculum and in arriving at a correct evaluation of the community's needs. The manner in which this controversial issue is treated will have far-reaching effects upon school and community relationships.

Case Number Seven represents an example of the advantages of a comprehensive high school. In Case Number Eight some of the problems of the faculty of specialized high schools are described; these problems also may affect the students.

Case Number Seven—Canoe

Canoe has been a comprehensive high school for only two years. Prior to that time it was the local high school of a village of some 500 population. Its curriculum had been restricted, owing to its small enrollment and limited funds, to offering a college-preparatory program. Few electives were available, and, because of the small number from which to select, students had had a difficult time working them into their schedules.

After five years of suggestions for consolidation by the state department of education and employed consultants, the county of Canoe had voted to combine eight small high schools into one large, comprehensive school, Canoe. Canoe High was centrally located in the largest village within the county, which eliminated any serious transportation problems.

Under the new organization, Canoe High School offered three programs—college preparatory, general education, and vocational education. Pupils were able to take courses in areas other than their major program. This provision alone more than doubled the electives available to Canoe High School pupils. Students who desired vocational education no longer had to travel long distances to the one school which formerly offered this training, and Canoe was now large enough so that special classes could be established in mathematics, science, and language for the more advanced students.

In addition to these advantages, Canoe provided an opportunity for pupils of different cultural levels to attend school on the same campus. The first year of operation found parents hesitant to identify with the new school or to give up their attachment to the old schools, but citizens and pupils from feeder communities soon developed a sense of pride in Canoe High and lost any desire they may have had to return to the eight small, isolated schools of the past.

Case Number Eight—Technical High School

Technical High School was one of the earliest schools established in this metropolitan area. It was rich in pride and history. Included in its offerings were all the courses usually associated with a specialized school of this type. In addition, it provided some vocational education. Graduates of this school were well known and readily accepted for employment by those aware of the quality of its specialized training.

In the early part of its history, Technical High was very selective in admitting students. Later, its curriculum was expanded, and pupils of a more vocational interest were admitted. Along with this expansion of curriculum came less acceptance by the general public, who remembered it when it was specialized and preferred it to be selective.

Although specialization in Technical High had been reduced little if any, many citizens thought that the addition of vocational education had brought about a weakening of specialized training and a downgrading in faculty. Unfortunately, pupils shared this same feeling to some degree, and motivation of pupils became more difficult than previously. Pupils in the vocational-education phase were stigmatized as being of lower quality than those graduating from the college-preparatory high schools.

Questions for Discussion

Case Number One

1. Why did Steeltown not add music to its curriculum?

2. What could have been done to change the opinion of the local board of education? As superintendent, what would you have done?

Case Number Two

3. What was wrong with the attitude of the parents in establishing mathematics and science as requirements for high-school graduation?

4. What should determine the scope of the curriculum? Why? How could this have been handled more effectively?

Case Number Three

5. What factors determined the curriculum at Noble High School? Should consolidation be considered? Why?

6. If you had been the principal, what action would you have taken? Defend your point of view.

Case Number Four

7. Do you feel that the curriculum is determined in a desirable manner at Price Elementary School? Why?

8. What suggestions can you offer for the improvement of curriculum building? Who should determine what curriculums are offered?

Case Number Five

9. In what ways are the school experiences of children beneficial in an organization such as Deep Run Elementary School?

10. What are its disadvantages? Could these be eliminated? How?

Case Number Six

11. What are the advantages of organizing an elementary school on the basis on which Palm School was organized?

12. Do you visualize any disadvantages in this type of organization? Could these be removed?

Case Number Seven

13. What do you think of Canoe High School?

14. What are its advantages and disadvantages in terms of curriculum for high-school youth? Which type of high school do you prefer? Why?

Case Number Eight

15. What advantages do you see for high-school youth who attend Technical High School?

16. Why did some parents feel that it was losing prestige with the general public? Were they right?

17. Could this have been avoided? What would you do, if you were principal of Technical High School, to improve its present status?

Selected Readings

Anderson, Vernon E., *Principles and Procedures of Curriculum Improvement,* The Ronald Press Company, New York, 1956.

Conant, James B., *Education and Liberty,* Harvard University Press, Cambridge, Mass., 1953.

Daugherty, James H., Gorman, Frank H., and Phillips, Claudett, *Elementary School Organization and Management,* The Macmillan Company, New York, 1950.

Grant, Eva H., *Parents and Teachers as Partners,* Science Research Associates, Inc., Chicago, 1952.

Hand, Harold C., *What People Think About Their Schools,* World Book Company, Yonkers, N.Y., 1948.

Hymes, James L., *Effective Home-School Relations,* Prentice-Hall, Inc., Englewood Cliffs, N.J., 1953.

Jones, James J., "The Superintendent Must Lead in Curriculum Development," *Educational Administration and Supervision,* **45:** 91–94, March, 1959.

Keller, Franklin J., *The Comprehensive High School,* Harper & Brothers, New York, 1955.

Kindred, Leslie W., *School Public Relations,* Prentice-Hall, Inc., Englewood Cliffs, N.J., 1957.

Langdon, Grace, and Stout, Irving W., *Helping Parents Understand Their Child's School,* Prentice-Hall, Inc., Englewood Cliffs, N.J., 1957.

McCloskey, Gordon, "How to Reach Your Public," *School Executive,* **77:** 54–57, March, 1958.

McCloskey, Gordon, *Education and Public Understanding,* Harper & Brothers, New York, 1959.

Martin, William O., *The Order and Integration of Knowledge,* University of Michigan Press, Ann Arbor, 1957.

Nielander, William A., and Miller, Raymond W., *Public Relations,* The Ronald Press Company, New York, 1951.

Pierce, Truman M., Merrill, Ward C., Jr., Wilson, L. Craig, and Kimbrough, Ralph B., *Community Leadership for Public Education,* Prentice-Hall, Inc., Englewood Cliffs, N.J., 1955.

Stout, Irving W., and Langdon, Grace, "What Parents Want to Know About Their Child's School," *Nation's Schools,* **60:** 45–48, August, 1957.

ISSUES DEALING WITH INSTRUCTION

7.

THROUGH legally established boards of education, our citizens have founded schools and staffed them with professional personnel to guide the growth and development of their children, physically, socially, emotionally, and intellectually. Public schools exist for the purpose of teaching pupils, and not to give positions to administrators and teachers. The school plant, budget, and services are only aids to the big job, which is instruction. Before any change is made in any program or activity, the administrator must ask himself, "How does this affect instruction?"

The core of any school public-relations program starts with this point in mind. What takes place daily in each classroom is of paramount importance to parents and taxpayers.

Perhaps there is no medium of public relations as effective as excellent teaching by every teacher. All other school activities are inextricably woven in and around this experience. Parents send their children to school to learn. They want to know what is being taught. Parents want to know how their child is doing at school in adjustment, achievement, and study skills.

The issues dealing with instruction are so numerous and

complex that it is possible to treat only a limited number here. The major considerations in this chapter are given to grouping for instruction, homework for pupils, discipline, and the broad area of grading, reporting, and promotion.

How Should Pupils Be Grouped for Instruction?

Traditionally, children have been grouped by chronological age since, obviously, there is a general relationship between age and physical and intellectual development. Children, however, do differ in such development. Not only may a child's physical, social, emotional, and intellectual development differ from that of other children, but his own pace of development may vary in each area. It is not hard to understand the complexities existing here. The issue is packed with emotional implications. Parents and children can accept without too much difficulty the fact that one child is larger than another, or that one is better in music, or that one is more socially adaptable, or that one has better control of his temper, but it is extremely hard for a parent or child to accept the fact that another child is intellectually superior.

Almost since the beginning of public education, chronological age has been used as a basis for classifying and grouping pupils. It has been an administratively convenient method and one which parents are not too likely to argue against. It has been customary for many years that children begin school in the first grade at age six, although it has been established that children, with some exceptions, are more likely to learn to read at age six and one half than at six. So many factors enter into reading readiness, such as maturation, environment, and physical health, that a hard and fast rule for grade or chronological age is difficult to defend. Although many state laws and state-board regulations are too inflexible to permit administrative adjustments, with our present knowledge of child development, further study should be given to this method of grouping.

Ability grouping was used widely during the early part of the twentieth century, and recently there has been some evidence of recurring interest in it. Early efforts at ability grouping were based largely on results of intelligence and achievement tests. More recently, average scholarship marks in all subjects, teachers' rating of students' academic ability, and scores from prognostic tests have been added as criteria.

Ability grouping is sometimes attacked as being undemocratic, unrealistic, and inconsistent with a modern educational program. Critics contend that it does not implement the educational concept of well-rounded development for individual students and does not provide for the mixing of pupils with high-level intelligence with those of lower level. They further contend that bright pupils tend to develop a "halo" effect about their own status and that pupils in a "slow" group often have feelings of inferiority. It is also said that there is little evidence that schools using ability grouping can deal more effectively with individual pupil needs than schools which use some form of heterogeneous grouping. A basic strength of this method of grouping, however, is that it tends to group on the basis of relatively unchangeable traits which signify the probable learning rate of pupils. Care, of course, must be exercised to adapt instruction to selected abilities.

Contrary to widely held opinion, homogeneous and ability grouping are not the same. Homogeneous grouping takes into consideration a number of factors other than intellectual capacity and achievement. It seeks to group pupils who are similar in ability, age, persistence, previous experience, general like-mindedness, and other factors which affect learning. Of course, it is understood that it is impossible to have a *completely* homogeneous group.

In its extreme form, heterogeneous grouping seeks the opposite of homogeneous grouping: it attempts to distribute the bright, average, and slow learners throughout the various classes and grades, in the belief that pupils learn from each other as well as from the teacher. No child, regardless of his aptitude and achievement, possesses all the skills of all subjects taught in school; children on each level may learn from children on any other level. Good attitudes and human relations can be taught by pupils as well as teachers.

Unfortunately, not enough research and experimentation have been done to determine with any degree of finality if any method or combination of grouping methods is best for all pupils. Many different types of grouping have been tried, with varying degrees of alleged successes. Some of the types have been accepted by parents, whereas others have not.

Case Number One depicts the use of ability grouping as tried in selected classes in one particular school. It indicates some of the difficulties one may find in using this type of grouping.

Case Number Two illustrates the use of an ungraded school to solve an unusual problem in a local area.

Case Number One—Baker School

Baker School is composed of grades one through twelve, with the first six grades being considered a part of the elementary school. Two main buildings house the pupils, grades one to six being in one and grades seven to twelve in the other. The wealth of this school area is well above average for the state.

Although the pupils in the elementary grades had always

been grouped by grades or grouped within the grades for special subjects, depending upon the individual teacher, the elementary-school principal and faculty decided to try an experiment for one year with ability grouping. They grouped the pupils in the upper three grades, three to six, as nearly as possible on the basis of ability. Intelligence tests, achievement tests, average scholarship marks in all subjects, teacher's ratings of the students' academic ability, and scores from a prognostic test were used as the bases for dividing the pupils into three groups within each grade.

At the end of the academic year, the teachers were asked to evaluate the experiment. The majority indicated that they felt the over-all effect was not good. They did feel that the strengths of ability grouping lay in the high-level instruction and learning that was possible for the top group. Responses indicated, however, that these strengths were more than offset by the attitude of snobbery which many of the pupils exhibited at school. Comments such as the following were not uncommon: "Are you in the bright group, the average group, or the dumb group?" Some of the pupils in the slow groups did not show as much progress as they had in previous years when they were otherwise grouped, and all of them resented the slow-group label.

Some of the teachers were disappointed in their own inability to meet the individual needs of pupils as well as they had predicted under this system of grouping. A careful study of faculty responses and faculty discussion of the relative merits of various patterns of grouping resulted in the principal and faculty deciding to return to the grade grouping formerly used.

Case Number Two—Long School

Long School is located in an area inhabited for several months each year by migrant workers. The main type of work performed by these people is harvesting of crops grown by truck farmers and gathering of cotton during the early fall. Long School is supported by the county school district.

A major problem confronting the principal and faculty is the grouping of pupils for instruction. Enrollment is grades one to eight at Long School varied from approximately 200 in September to 500 during the busiest harvest season, and it was difficult to find well-trained faculty willing to work on a part-time basis. Many of the pupils came back to the same school each year during the harvest season, but, at most, their length of stay would be three to four months. These pupils lived with their migrant parents in trailers under deplorable conditions, disease and poverty being common elements of their lives. To complicate the problem further, the majority of the transient children spoke either Spanish or German and were very deficient in English. The language barrier plus a lack of information about the children's previous schooling made it almost impossible to place them in their proper grades.

It was obvious to the faculty and principal that this school needed some method of grouping for instruction other than chronological age or grade. After careful study of the problem and with assistance from the local state university, it was decided to use a weighted combination of mental age, physical development, social maturity, and emotional maturity to supplement what data were available. Each child was interviewed individually after these data were collected during his first week at school. Then the pupil was placed in a group that most nearly met his individual needs, a grouping that had very little to do with age. Letter symbols were used for the groups, but their precise meaning was kept from the children. As individuals progressed, they were moved to the next higher group for instruction, and some children were able to move through three to four groups per year when they attended regularly.

Despite the many problems still existing in the school, the faculty likes this ungraded plan better than any other it has tried; they believe it is the best possible one for solving their very special grouping problem.

Is There Value in Homework for Pupils?

Wide differences of opinion exist among parents, children, and teachers on this issue. Some feel that there should not be homework in certain grades, and some think that there should. Others feel there should be more homework than there is, and still others believe that the *kind* of homework is the important issue. Ideally, schoolwork should be so interesting and inviting that a child will want to take part of that work home with him. There is no question that this goal is sought and attained by many teachers.

Unfortunately, in some cases the only real contact many parents have with the school is through the homework their child brings home. From this the parents find out what the child is learning, how he or she is learning it, and what the teacher expects the child to learn. Homework, then, can be one of the best or poorest kinds of public-relations contact that a school can have. This is one medium that touches all homes. If homework is given, it should be the kind that tells parents that the school is interested in the child's learning.

Pupils who are given the most difficult homework assignments are sometimes the ones least able to handle them. For example, the high-school pupil with less than average ability who has difficulty in algebra may be assigned additional work because he is behind the rest of the class, and it may be just enough to discourage the pupil from doing any homework at all. There is little justification for homework of this type. If homework is to be used in teaching pupils, it should be motivated by what is best for the student. It must be reasonable in terms of requirements.

Some of the advantages claimed for homework include the following:

1. It helps parents to know what the school is teaching their child.

2. It encourages independent study on the part of the pupil.

3. Homework relates schoolwork to out-of-school life.

4. Homework enables pupils to try out new ideas on their own without close supervision from the teacher.

5. It can aid pupils who are about average in ability, and who possess perseverance, to catch up with other pupils who do classwork much faster.

6. It provides opportunity for pupils to learn to follow directions which were given at school.

Some of the disadvantages claimed for homework include the following:

1. Parents, rather than the child, frequently do the homework.

2. Pupils may stay up late at night in order to complete home assignments and thus go to school the next day without adequate rest.

3. The slow student is often further discouraged because of extra homework assigned to him.

4. It competes with other activities in which children are expected to participate outside of school hours.

5. Many homes do not provide satisfactory working con-

ditions for learning; presence of smaller children, family television viewing, poor lighting, and so on, can be distracting factors.

6.   Much of the homework assigned pupils is too difficult to encourage independent study.

7.   The purpose of homework is often not made clear to the pupils.

Studies of the homework question have sought to discover the attitudes of pupils, parents, and teachers toward homework and the kinds of homework assigned. Strangely enough, pupils and parents have expressed less condemnation of homework than have educators.

Homework in the elementary grades, especially the primary grades, has not been as successful as it has in the upper elementary grades and in high school. It is rather difficult to get immature children to work on independent assignments. The attention span of children in the first three grades is especially limited, but as children progress through the grades homework becomes less difficult.

For homework to be meaningful, it should be of interest and concern to the pupil. He must understand what is expected of him at home in terms of preparation and how this fits into the school picture. Further, the pupil must be able to see some relationship between his home assignment and his future profession or career. Homework assignments should grow out of regular classwork and should be of assistance in developing independent study habits. The degree of understanding manifested by teachers in making homework assignments is a primary factor in its acceptance by pupils and parents.

Case Number Three is an example of homework which discourages pupils and irritates parents.

Case Number Four shows how homework which grows out

of class experiences and is geared to individual needs can be helpful.

Case Number Three—Mrs. Snow

Mrs. Snow was a teacher of mathematics in a small-town high school. She held both the bachelor's and master's degrees from a church-related private university. She was married but had no children. Mrs. Snow was very active in church and community life, her co-workers often describing her as "that bundle of nervous energy." She spent many hours in class preparation, and her high-school students felt that she knew her subject matter.

Mrs. Snow always prided herself in "pouring on the work." In a second-year algebra class she gave from three to four hours of homework each day. She did not stop with having pupils work three or four examples in each exercise; she wanted all the problems in the text under each exercise worked out every day. Since the school was small, she was the only mathematics teacher, and students at low as well as high levels of achievement were forced to take her class.

After two months of assigning heavy homework, Mrs. Snow lost her temper one Friday in class and assigned the tenth-grade algebra class 150 problems to be worked over the week end. Even the best students in the class resented this assignment. Mrs. Snow received many telephone calls from parents who objected to such unreasonable homework, and several parents called the principal. They felt that this type of homework was punishment and lacked educational purpose. They further contended that Mrs. Snow gave homework to create the impression that she was a "tough" teacher, one who expected high standards.

Most of the parents refused to help their children complete

this assignment, and on Monday only two out of the class of thirty-eight had done any homework at all. A dozen parents accompanied their children to school and demanded to see the principal. The principal invited Mrs. Snow to meet with him and the angry parents. After long hours of talk, much debate, and some thinking, it was agreed that the children could forget this particular home assignment. The principal suggested that he and Mrs. Snow would talk over the situation further and attempt to arrive at a more workable solution concerning homework and promised to have the entire faculty study the homework question at its next faculty meeting to see if some new general policies could be developed.

Case Number Four—Mr. Gold

Mr. Gold taught social studies in a high school located in a large city. He held the bachelor's and master's degrees from the local state university and was in his tenth year of teaching. He read widely and was known by his co-workers as an excellent social-studies teacher. Owing to his success as a teacher, he was well known in the school area, despite the fact that it comprised many square miles.

Homework assignments made by Mr. Gold often called for parental involvement. On one occasion Mr. Gold assigned an eighth-grade civics class the task of finding out what their parents thought about America's race with Russia to conquer outer space. Each pupil was instructed to ask a series of ten questions of each parent and return to class the next day prepared to quote their parents' answers and their reasons for these answers. This homework grew out of a class discussion concerning outer space and who should control it. One boy stated, "My father does not think our government is spending enough money for missile development." Another pupil said,

"My mother thinks we should spend more money for atomic research and less for missiles."

The discussion found each pupil eager to give his results and to tell why his parents believed as they did. The children were also happy to see their parents' opinions given serious consideration.

Mr. Gold received more than a dozen telephone calls the following day from parents who expressed delight that their children were getting an opportunity to discuss current national affairs. The principal was told by a number of parents at the next PTA meeting about Mr. Gold's fine homework assignments and how much they appreciated them.

Is Discipline Related to Self-Direction?

Parents want to be sure that their child is in a classroom where respect for others exists. They are concerned about reports of freedom without the responsibilities that should go with freedom. Parents want to be assured that the school is holding a reasonably tight rein on behavior; even parents who allow excessive freedoms at home are likely to expect controls at school. Parents are equally concerned, of course, with the possibility that school controls may be too harsh, and few parents favor any form of corporal punishment in the schools.

The concept of discipline which may be defined as "classroom order," one in which the teacher takes advantage of his position of authority to force others to do what he wishes, allows for little self-direction. This "take my word for it" type of classroom control lacks the essential elements necessary for an environment conducive to learning. Under this theory the purpose of discipline is simply to prevent disorder.

This type of discipline has many dangers. It is easy for the teacher to resort to some type of punishment which pupils fear, without having given her full attention to its total effect upon their behavior. It may cause the teacher to avoid understanding the real attitudes which are being built as a result of this type of discipline. Perhaps more important is the fact that the cause of the undesirable behavior is not ascertained or removed.

A wise understanding of the genetic development of children is necessary in order to understand their behavior. Treatment of misconduct should seek to inspire the pupil to right action rather than merely to restrain him from bad behavior. Disciplinary measures should aim chiefly at modifying undesirable social actions rather than as punishment for an offense.[1] Discipline is closely connected with motivation. A positive attitude toward children will succeed in most classrooms, whereas a negative attitude will likely create new problems. All teachers should be certain that any disciplinary action taken by them is to bring about a redirection of behavior in the child and not to relieve their own tensions.

Children are developing organisms and will manifest behavior tendencies, from time to time, which are inconsistent. Teachers know that many things done by children which are annoying to adults are to be expected of young people. The teacher should not express surprise over minor offenses; when these offenses are ignored, children are less likely to repeat them. Effective control of problems requires that the teacher be as objective as possible in dealing with them; even though offenses may be directed at her personally, she should not imply in any way that she considers them in that light. The teacher who permits herself to feel that a child's offense is a personal affront is not in a position to assume the role of an

---

[1] See James J. Jones, "Guidance of Pupil Behavior," *Journal of the National Education Association,* 43: 176, March, 1954.

impartial judge and is not likely to give due heed to the child's side of the question.

Successful leadership of children demands that the teacher realize the pupil's needs for opportunity to release his store of energy through some worthwhile activity. A constructive way to provide for this natural urge is to provide for many activities in the classrooms. The teacher should plan her work well and never be caught by the students in a position where she is trying to decide what they should do next. A child's energies will find an outlet; it is up to the teacher to see that the outlet is constructive, not mischievous. Discipline, at its peak performance, assists the individual in the establishment of desirable habits of social living. This concept really regards discipline as a problem of growth by the learner. This growth develops from a state of great dependence to the point where a child accepts the responsibility for his own behavior or self-direction. Good discipline is self-discipline, whether in school or in life. A wealth of evidence points to the fact that the use of effective teaching procedures is the most certain guarantee of success in the guidance of pupil behavior.

Case Number Five illustrates a type of discipline that has its emphasis upon preventing disorder.

Case Number Six illustrates discipline used to modify undesirable social behavior rather than to serve as punishment for misbehavior.

Case Number Five—Mr. Exact

Mr. Exact was a teacher of science in a secondary school in a small mining town. He had received his bachelor's degree from a small liberal-arts college some twenty years before, and had later taken twelve semester hours in professional education for certification. He really did not think very much of professional training, and therefore put little into it and received very little in return. Mr. Exact felt that knowing one's subject matter and passing on this knowledge to children was the entire teaching process in a "nutshell." Further, Mr. Exact felt that pupils came to school to be seen and not necessarily heard. It was his feeling that pupils could not learn in a classroom without there being absolute quiet at all times, a situation he called "good classroom order."

Although the pupils understood that Mr. Exact expected perfect peace and quiet, they did, on occasion, check out his rigid rules to see how far he would go to enforce them. One hot spring day the senior class was having a study period in a chemistry class, and Mr. Exact was called from the room for a few minutes. Before leaving, he issued this dictum: "Any student who has not completed his assigned work by the end of this period will have to stay after school and do an additional assignment." Because resentment had been building up for a long time, the class president got up after the teacher left and asked the class to skip the day's assignment. After all, what could the teacher do if they all refused to do the assignment. This undesirable attitude on the part of the class was, of course, a way of getting back at Mr. Exact.

Upon his return, Mr. Exact flew into a rage and made rash threats. The pupils burst out into laughter and got up and left the classroom when the bell rang for the end of the period. When Mr. Exact talked with the principal about the matter, he learned that the pupils in a number of his other classes also resented his highhandedness but had not expressed themselves before. The principal scheduled additional conferences with Mr. Exact to discuss proper ways of obtaining classroom discipline.

Case Number Six—Miss Frank

Miss Frank taught fifth grade in a modern building where the faculty had a general agreement about how discipline was to be used in connection with children. She had taught for more than ten years in the same room and in the same school. Miss Frank held both the bachelor's and master's degrees from a state college. She had done additional work and had received an advanced diploma from the state university. Miss Frank was very active in professional groups and a constant student of better ways of teaching.

One year Miss Frank experienced some difficulty in getting her pupils to walk to the lunchroom quietly. Many of them came from a new suburban area and had not attended this school before. Although the children were instructed to go to the lunchroom in groups of two and three, there were several who insisted on making noise and disturbing other classes. Recognizing this type of experience as being new for these pupils, Miss Frank took some time out from other classwork to talk with the group about why they should not disturb others. In addition, she talked with the pupils who gave the most trouble and told them that she knew they could show the rest of the group how to go to the lunchroom without disturbing others. For almost two weeks, for about ten minutes prior to lunch, the entire class discussed the problem of going to the lunchroom quietly, and suggestions were made by pupils as to why quiet was desirable and what would be the best way to achieve it. Before long, all unnecessary noise in the lunch line had been eliminated.

How Are Grading, Reporting, and Promotion Related to Instruction?

Parents are interested in the grades which their children receive at school. First, it is helpful to consider the purposes of grades. One reason for grades is that some type of information is necessary to determine whether pupils pass or fail a particular course. A second reason is to inform the teacher, pupil, and parents of the pupil's success or lack of it in a subject or given class. Grades can also be diagnostic: the teacher can learn about the pupil's strengths and weaknesses in order to guide him and his work along satisfactory lines. A fourth reason for grades is to provide a record of a school's achievements.

Grades should not be allowed to become the major incentive to pupil effort. Grades should not be used as threats or as a bonus for good work. A good teacher wants his pupils to study for the satisfaction gained from the learning experience and not for grades. Grades should be a means to an end, not an end in themselves.

Irrespective of the system of marking or grading used within a school, pupils and parents want to know what the grading symbols mean and how they are derived. They want to know if the grade is based upon a comparison with other students in the same class or with national norms, or if it is based upon individual progress.

Many parents want their children all to make the highest grade. This desire has prompted some parents to apply undue pressure on their children, who, in a few instances, lack the necessary ability to make superior grades. This lack of understanding on the part of parents creates problems for their children and the school. Making high grades requires more than hard work. It requires a desire and a capacity for learning the various tasks expected in schoolwork.

The primary purpose in reporting pupil grades is to inform the parent and the pupil about his progress in school. Parents object to reports that tell very little about their child, and it is the job of the school to make reports to parents useful and meaningful. Among the many different forms of reports to parents, each has its own particular advantage, and no one report is best for all schools, whether it be a report card or booklet, a narrative or letter report, a conference between the parent and the teacher, or a combination of these three.

Although the faults of the traditional report card are generally known, a majority of the schools still use it. The trend, however, seems to be toward supplementing the card with other types of reports in order to give a more complete account.

One common method used to replace or supplement the traditional report card is the narrative report, which may vary from a small space on a report card to a rather lengthy informal letter. When properly used, the narrative form is a good method for describing individual differences and providing an interrelated picture of social, emotional, physical, and scholastic conditions. Unfortunately, many teachers do not have sufficient skill to use this form correctly. Also, teachers may hesitate to be critical of a pupil's faults for fear of antagonizing his parents. Then, too, long narrative reports are time consuming and tend to overburden teachers and to lead to faulty reporting.

One very effective method of reporting fully on the progress of a child is the parent-teacher conference. If the home and the school are to cooperate in the responsibility for a child's development, the personal contacts provided by conferences can be very helpful. Some of the disadvantages of other methods of reporting can be eliminated by the face-to-face relationships of conferences.

Any system of marking and reporting has its advantages and disadvantages, but it is possible to avoid some faults by combining different methods. Many schools are now using more than one method of reporting and find the combination advantageous.

There are few conditions in life that upset parents and teachers, as well as pupils, to the extent that nonpromotion does. Parents are deeply concerned about their child's progress from grade to grade. Promotion is a powerful incentive to a student.

The cost of failure is great—to the pupil, to the school system, and to society. The causes of failure or nonpromotion in schools are numerous, including low mentality, lack of interest, lack of effort, illness, excessive absences, and poor study habits. It may well be that some of these causes are brought about by the school itself. These include overcrowded classes, curriculum inadequacies, lack of guidance services, incompetent instruction, and lack of special assistance. Home and community environment may also contribute to nonpromotion.

In order to develop a promotional policy that has meaning for pupils, parents, and faculty, a number of considerations should be made. First, it is necessary to recognize that individual differences do exist and that no type of instruction can make pupils come to the same achievement level in all areas at the same time. Second, it makes little difference where pupils are placed as long as teachers take them from their present status and attempt to raise them to higher planes of learning. Third, improvement in achievement is very closely related to a student's growth, which includes social, emotional, and physical factors.

It is doubtful if anyone would argue that all children should be promoted regardless of achievement. Many of the concepts presented, however, apply more readily to the elementary school than to the secondary school, for it is in the elementary school that a majority of failures take place. In some instances children have been retained because of poor work in one subject when, actually, the child was doing well in five or six others. The question might be raised, "Who has failed, the teacher, the pupil, or the school?" A minimum recommendation would be for the teacher, the pupil, the parents, and the principal to sit down together and discuss a child's strengths and weaknesses before the pupil is retained.

Case Number Seven illustrates the use of grades to threaten students.

Case Number Eight illustrates how a nonpromotion policy was revised in the light of new information.

Case Number Seven—Mrs. Dickey

Mrs. Dickey had taught elementary grades for more than twelve years. Her background and training were considered excellent, and her relationships with peers were good. Mrs. Dickey was, in many ways, a perfectionist. Her pupils never seemed to be able to do enough work to please her.

One year she was assigned to a group of fourth-grade pupils that gave her much difficulty. Many of the children in her grade were of average intelligence, but more than half of the particular group could be classed as dull normal. On one occasion Mrs. Dickey gave a very difficult assignment in arithmetic and expected the pupils to come to class prepared, but they were unable to work the problems either at home or at school. She then reassigned the same material for the next day and threatened the entire class with failing grades if the work was not completed. Some of the parents of the children visited the school to discuss the arithmetic assignments. Mrs. Dickey was immediately on the defensive and stated, "These pupils must learn to do the work that I assign if they expect to make a passing grade." The parents talked with the principal. Finally, a conference was arranged with the parents, the teacher, and the principal. The outcome was that Mrs. Dickey agreed to amend her assignment and to reappraise her use of grades.

Case Number Eight—Mr. Moses

Mr. Moses taught fourth grade in a large elementary school in the city where he was born and grew up. He had received excellent training for the teaching profession and was working part time on his doctorate degree. The School in which Mr. Moses taught did not promote students if they failed one main subject within a grade. While Mr. Moses was pursuing his doctorate at the local state university, he did a piece of individual research on promotional theories for the elementary schools. Out of this research came some ideas which were of great help in clarifying his own thinking. Mr. Moses showed the results of his study to his principal, who suggested that the faculty might wish to consider using this material for professional discussions.

The faculty accepted the suggestion, and a committee was formed to conduct a study of the effects of nonpromotion in their school. At the end of the school year the faculty agreed that the following year the promotional policies would be to promote every child whenever possible. It was also decided that teachers should carefully consider chronological age, mental maturity, social experience, scholastic achievement, and the hopes, aims, and attitudes of the pupil before reaching a decision on retaining him.

Questions for Discussion

Case Number One

1. What were the strong points in the use of ability grouping in Baker School?

2. Do you think the evidence is sufficient for a discontinuance of this form of grouping? Why?

Case Number Two

3. What are the advantages of the ungraded school used in this case? What are the disadvantages?

4. How would you have handled this problem had you been principal?

Case Number Three

5. If you were principal of the school in this case, what action would you have taken?

6. Assume that you are a parent of a child involved in this controversy over homework. What action would you take?

Case Number Four

7. In what way did Mr. Gold show insight into pupil needs?

8. Evaluate Mr. Gold's homework assignment.

9. Do you have other suggestions for improvement?

Case Number Five

10. Do you agree with Mr. Exact about the purpose of discipline? Why?

11. What suggestions could you give Mr. Exact for improvement concerning the guidance of pupil behavior?

Case Number Six

12. What do you think is the purpose of discipline in this case?

13. Compare this case with Case Number Five.

14. What suggestions do you have for Miss Frank?

Case Number Seven

15. Do you agree with Mrs. Dickey about the purpose of grades? Why?

16. Should parental pressure be considered in a case like this? why?

17. What suggestions do you have for Mrs. Dickey?

Case Number Eight

18. What do you think of the role Mr. Moses played?

19. Do you agree with the policies developed and put into practice by this school?

20. Can you think of exceptions to the policies adopted in this case?

Selected Readings

Cook, W. W., "Some Effects of Maintenance of High Standards of Promotion," *Eementary School Journal,* **41**: 430–437, February, 1951.

Jones, James J., "Guidance of Pupil Behavior," *Journal of the National Education Association,* **43**: 176, March, 1954.

Jones, James J., "Recent Trends in Promotion Policies," *Progressive Education,* **33**: 5–6, 15, January, 1956.

Jones, James J., "Methods of Reporting to Parents," *Virginia Journal of Education,* **50**: 11, 50–51, October, 1956.

Lafferty, H. M., "Reasons for Pupil Failure," *American School Board Journal,* **117**: 18–20, July, 1948.

Langdon, Grace, and Stout, Irving W., *Helping Parents Understand Their Child's School,* Prentice-Hall, Inc., Englewood Cliffs, N.J., 1957.

McDougall, Curtis D., *Understanding Public Opinion,* The Macmillan Company, New York, 1952.

National School Public Relations Association, *Public Relations*

Gold Mine, National Education Association, Washington, D.C., 1957.

Rothney, John W. M., *Evaluating and Reporting Pupil Progress,* No. 7 in What Research Says to the Teacher Series, National Education Association, Dept. of Classroom Teachers, Washington, D.C., 1955.

Stout, Irving W., and Langdon, Grace, *Parent-Teacher Relationships,* No. 16 in What Research Says to the Teacher Series, National Education Association, Dept. of Classroom Teachers, Washington, D.C., 1958.

Strang, Ruth, *Reporting to Parents,* Bureau of Publications, Teachers College, Columbia University, New York, 1947.

Wrightstone, J. Wayne, *Class Organization for Instruction,* No. 13 in What Research Says to the Teacher Series, National Education Association, Dept. of Classroom Teachers, Washington, D.C., 1955.

ISSUES DEALING WITH COMMUNITY GROUPS

8.

IN THE organization and development of educational programs, administrators work with many persons and groups. These groups, in each community, are numerous and varied. Their functions are likewise multifarious. In every community there are organized groups capable of contributing to the development of school public relations. In small communities some groups have proportionately greater influence and power than their fellow organizations in large communities, where greater diversity and competition of outside interests tend to restrict the power of any single group. It is significant for the administrator to know what groups exist in his community. He should know how to find these groups and how each does its work. He should learn the objectives of each group and how the groups are interrelated.

In order to secure these data, it may be necessary to do a thorough sociological analysis of the community. This type of study goes far beyond the limited kind of routine survey which is frequently made of a community. A detailed study of the school and community should help to identify areas of ignorance. This may involve areas in which the school lacks understanding of the community, or ones in which the community fails to understand the school. After these areas are identified, it is possible to establish an organized program of public relations that may include suggestions for constructing better relations between the receptive schools and communities.

The list of organized community groups is almost endless; therefore, no attempt is made to study or to evaluate their total effectiveness; rather, the purpose of this chapter is to pinpoint the issues which are closely identified with school public relations and to discuss their implications. Included in this vast array of issues are the parent-teacher association, the citizen advisory committee, and public opinion versus professional opinion.

To What Extent Do Parent-Teacher Associations Promote School Public Relations?

It has become increasingly clear, as the study of education has developed, that the child is influenced by experiences outside of the school as well as by those in it. The child's experiences outside of the school may aid his school development, neutralize it, or contradict it. A teacher can work more effectively if he knows something of the experiences of the child when not in school. Changes in the home environment can affect the child's behavior in school.

The amount and quality of understanding that parents have concerning child growth and development are of vital importance in operating an effective school program. Recognition of this concept has led to a demand for more education of parents. It is no longer adequate for parents to build a good home environment; they should also know how to work with teachers and to supply them with needed data about the child. Parents need suggestions as to what experiences at home can help the child do better work at school. Joint efforts on the part of parents and teachers are necessary if the child is to enjoy maximum satisfaction.

Perhaps the best-known and the most widely used organization which attempts to solve problems dealing with parent-teacher relationships is the parent-teacher association. The parent-teacher association is a volunteer organization composed of teachers and parents of a particular school. The general purpose of the local association is to improve the effectiveness of the school. The majority of these organizations are affiliated with state associations and with the National Congress of Parents and Teachers.

The effectiveness of local units varies from those providing excellent support for public education to others which oppose many of the things that the school is doing. As in every undertaking which involves the school, the effectiveness of activities needs to be ascertained from time to time.

A synthesis of the arguments for and against the work of the parent-teacher association provides some insight into its success and difficulties.

The Parent-Teacher Association in this country has many accomplishments to its credit. It has stood the test of time and can be classed as a stable organization. Its origin dates to the founding of the National Congress of Mothers, in 1897, by Alice Birney and Phoebe Hearst. This association gives parents an opportunity to learn what teachers are trying to do for their children. It has carried on excellent programs of parent education through planned study programs and through the organization and development of "grade mothers." The association has aided school districts in obtaining public opinion on selected issues and in carrying out pupil-population studies which helped the administrator and school board plan for educational facilities.

Likewise, teachers are afforded the opportunity to learn about parents and the homes of the children. A large number of parents have learned to enjoy additional knowledge about the school and the teacher. They feel a sense of satisfaction in being able to be a small part of an up-to-date and ongoing social institution. The parent-teacher association at the national level publishes *The National Parent Teacher*. This excellent journal for parents is published monthly, September through June. It provides a wealth of data for both parents and teachers.

Although there are many strengths which have been mentioned concerning the parent-teacher association, of equal importance are its limitations, and these should be recognized. Not all parents who belong to the association are happy with their relationship. Many parents join because it is their response to a sense of duty; they feel that they should belong. Some are members because of repeated requests on the part of their children, the teachers, and other parents.

Another limitation is the lack of quality in many of the monthly programs, which often are rigid and noninformative, and provide a captive audience for some speaker who has been invited to talk without remuneration. The overdependence upon the PTA to do everything has, in some instances, caused other local-interest groups to be silenced. Combined with this limitation is the fact that the association is not very successful in getting parents of the upper elementary grades and high school to be active members, which makes its representation of the community rather poor. Many middle-aged and elderly parents are not represented in this association. Despite the large membership claimed for this organization, many of its members are not active. In fact, the inactivity of so many people has a retarding effect upon the school personnel and the leaders of the association. Another cause for complaint has come from administrators and teachers who feel that the kind and types of activity which associations undertake are not always desirable. The primary function of a PTA is not to raise money for some school cause, to seek to direct the school, or to make policy. The function of the parent-teacher association is advisory in nature. When local associations lose sight of the objectives of the National Congress of Parents and Teachers, it is likely that they are engaging in activities which are inappropriate for them.

A wealth of evidence supports the many possible advantages of the PTA. It is incumbent upon the school administrator to play an important role in helping to clarify the work of the association. He should work closely with the organization and encourage it to engage in worthwhile activities. It is his job to help but not to dominate. The PTA has many potential leaders whose qualities of leadership can add immeasurably to good public education and to public relations.

Case Number One illustrates how one parent-teacher association encouraged parents to visit the school and made certain they had opportunities to learn about the school and their children.

Case Number Two illustrates a parent-teacher association engaging in activities not appropriate for promoting better parent-teacher relationships.

Case Number One—Silver Valley

Located in a wealthy mining area, Silver Valley Public High School had a wonderful school program. Its patrons and teachers recognized the value of a good educational program and did all possible to support it. One of the leading organized community groups was the parent-teacher association. The association had two presidents—a husband-and-wife combination. First and second vice presidents were also husband and wife.

The PTA adopted a theme for the year which emphasized the presentation of a wide and varied type of information to parents, one that encouraged parents to participate in the functions of its organization by learning about school activities. An example of the way this local unit educates parents and teachers is illustrated by the following PTA program.

Movies of selected scenes from a school basketball game were shown to the parents. Several large cardboard charts and tables were prepared to give parents and teachers an understanding of what it costs to have a basketball team—in terms of time, effort, and money. Additional information was provided about the interscholastic association, the salary of coaches, the training of basketball officials, the transportation of players, the type of equipment used, and the cost of insurance for players.

Members of the school publications department described the value of pre- and postgame publicity. The head of the audio-visual department demonstrated the use of the public-address system and explained that the student announcer who broadcasted the home games was receiving training in sports announcing. The cheerleaders gave data on their hours of practice, the cost of their uniforms, and the nature of the yells used at the games. Members of the coaching staff explained several basketball plays and demonstrated equipment available for school use. Parents and teachers were invited to ask questions and to make suggestions.

Case Number Two—Oceanview

The parents and teachers of Oceanview Elementary School, along with the principal, wanted a parent-teacher association the second year after the school was established. After an organizational meeting, a community group became known as the parent-teacher association. Immediately, the association began to conduct drives for membership. Classes were interrupted and pupils were requested to ask their parents to join the association. A number of women whose children were in school canvassed the community and secured more than two thirds of the parents as members. Some of these members paid the dues just to be rid of persons pestering them.

The first programs of the Oceanview Parent-Teacher Association attempted to work with the school personnel and administration to identify needs of the school. The group decided that the school needed a new motion-picture projector. A carnival was held under the sponsorship of the PTA for the purpose of raising funds for this machine. Bingo and other games of chance were used to raise more than $1,000. The principal purchased the projector and screen, and the school started showing films secured from the state department of education.

Later, some parents objected, on religious grounds, to the showing of certain films in the classroom. Other parents wanted to borrow the projector to use at home on weekends. Still others felt that the projector belonged to the association, although it had in reality been given to the school.

More dissension arose when a group of mothers, claiming to represent the PTA, insisted that they decide what kind of physical-education uniforms should be bought for the upper-elementary-grade pupils. They insisted that this was a duty of

PTA members and should not be left to the school personnel or physical-education instructors.

Program attendance began to fall off, and members who did attend said very little. The principal was not selected to be a member of the executive committee for the following year. The officers of the association informed the board of education of the poor cooperation being received from the principal and teachers. After two years of this type of operation, the principal requested that the PTA be discontinued.

Are Citizen Advisory Committees Desirable?

In many communities very little conscious effort is being expended to keep citizens up to date in matters concerning the functions of education and the possibilities of making schools more effective through use of new devices, techniques, and discoveries in the realm of practice. As a consequence, it is probable that the understanding of most people concerning the power of education is limited to their knowledge of the kinds of schools they themselves attended.

In many communities a large proportion of the citizens are parents, and they naturally have a keen interest in their children and, by being in close contact with the school, have developed a great understanding of the school's problems and difficulties. Parents whose children have already graduated from public schools often lose their keen interest in school activities because the challenge is no longer present, and they may tend to develop more of an indifferent attitude toward the needs of the school.

Still other parents send their children to private schools because they feel the public school is not doing a good job. This presents a real challenge to the administration and staff to contact these parents and work for their support, because their attitude is often antagonistic toward the public school.

A large percentage of the population in many communities are nonparents, and this constitutes a real problem in securing adequate support for the school. In most of our schools, very little consideration has been given to asking these people for their ideas and help in planning the school program or being of service in any other way, and, consequently, this group's over-all understanding of the school system suffers greatly— perhaps mostly through the school's own fault and indifference.

There is, consequently, a need for some type of lay advice. Citizen advisory committees may be called "citizens' advisory council," "lay advisory group," "public-school citizens' group," "national citizens' commission for public schools," and a host of other names.

A citizen advisory committee is a group of persons inside or outside the educational profession, chosen from the school staff or community to advise the school officials in regard to school programs. This body has no legal power but can offer its advice and recommendations to the legally constituted administrative officials. The major goal of such a group is to present responsible advice and points of view wherever they may be helpful. A second goal toward which this group may work is the collection and synthesis of public opinion concerning school problems. This type of assistance tends to prevent school administrators from being overwhelmed by information from a vocal minority.

Citizen advisory committees should not be thought of as a panacea for all the problems and criticisms of public education. Committees should not be initiated just to copy or follow what other school districts do. They must grow out of identified needs at the local level.

The following points are often made by those who favor the establishment of citizen advisory committees:

1. The interest level of parents and citizens today demands up-to-date information about schools.

2. Citizen participation aids the community in understanding, accepting, and encouraging the adoption of policies and programs.

3. Citizen advisory committees are an essential means of communication with the public about the school system.

4. Adults, like children, learn through taking part in some of the activities of the school.

5. Public participation strengthens local autonomy against bureaucracy.

6. Citizen advisory committees can be justified on the basis of consistency with the spirit of democracy.

Lay participation in educational planning also has certain disadvantages:

1. Lay persons are sometimes placed in positions where they are expected to make judgments concerning school procedures which they are unqualified to make.

2. Sometimes citizen advisory committees assume responsibilities and duties which belong to the board of education.

3. In selected instances, lay advisory committees have become pressure groups.

4. Some citizen groups are more concerned about lowering taxes, reducing the budget, and saving money than improving the schools.

5. Citizen advisory committees may become so efficient that the local board of education will depend upon them to do what should be its own thinking and interpretation.

6. The use of lay advisory committees often delays decisions.

Despite the many factors working for and against the use

of citizen advisory committees, the weight of the argument tends to favor their use. Of course it is wise to exercise certain cautions which have been mentioned here. In the long run, lay advice, if secured and used properly, will be helpful to most school systems and individual schools.

The example given in Case Number Three illustrates the use of a citizen advisory committee to assist the school board in its policy development. Case Number Four depicts a citizen group that is more interested in economy than in school improvements.

Case Number Three—Metropolitan County

Metropolitan County encompasses a city of some 350,000 population. The county school system has experienced a tremendous growth in pupil population during the past decade. Although the board of education has enjoyed long tenure in terms of its membership, many problems have arisen owing to the constant population increase. Many of the city workers reside in the county and commute to work. In many of the heavily populated sections of the county, neighbors do not know next-door neighbors except by their occupations or professions.

Several county parents requested that a kindergarten program be developed and paid for from the funds of the school district. The superintendent and the board of education looked with favor on the suggestion, but they knew that additional taxes would have to be levied to support such a program.

One of the school-board members, upon his return from the National School Boards Association convention where he learned of citizen advisory committees, proposed that such a committee be formed to work with the board of education and the administration. The board, with advice from the superintendent, appointed a lay committee to meet with it to study the needs of the county concerning a kindergarten program. The committee was fairly representative of the county and was composed of twenty-two members.

Working under the leadership of the superintendent and the board of education, this group of citizens developed an instrument and surveyed the citizens of the district on the kindergarten problem. Citizens were asked to indicate if they were interested in a kindergarten program and if they would be in favor of increased taxes to support it. The response was favorable, and a kindergarten program was put into operation. The board now meets with the advisory committee once a month, and the committee supports the administration and board by constantly explaining school policies and practices to the public.

Case Number Four—Eastburg

The principal of Eastburg Consolidated High School felt the need for help in the school's study of curriculums. He suggested to the faculty, and it accepted the idea, that five parents from each of the four high-school grades be selected by the home-room vote of the pupils to participate in the curriculum study. The twenty parents selected were to work with thirty faculty members to evaluate the curriculums. It was made clear to the parents that advisory committees could make suggestions but that the board of education would make final decisions on major changes.

The first month things seemed to go well, but during the second month the citizen group began to question everything, including the requirement that all high-school youth must take two years of physical education, which was a state law. As time passed, the group began to get out of hand. It started meeting on its own initiative and came to the regular biweekly meeting with suggestions it had developed independently. Next, the citizen group went to the superintendent's office and requested that its findings be presented to the board of education. It insisted that all classes of less than thirty enrollment be discontinued. It recommended that teachers be released if necessary, and that instructional costs be reduced. It wanted to do away with all art, music, and physical-education courses and to increase the number of foreign-language courses.

Because the citizen committe would neither cooperate nor work with the professional faculty, the principal asked the superintendent and board of education to be allowed to discontinue meeting with it. This permission was given, and the faculty and its principal continued the study without lay help.

Should Public Opinion Be Given Priority Over Professional Opinion?

From the beginning of public education in this country, it has been one of the functions of the school to work closely with its community and to keep communication lines open and free.

The deluge of criticisms leveled at education in recent years can almost make one believe that the public is completely dissatisfied with the American school system. Many of the criticisms have consisted of published viewpoints of individuals who have received much attention and have attracted many others to reply to their initial criticisms. As a result, opinion has been swayed and emotions have been fanned to the point where a discussion on public education can bring about a debate as hot as politics around any cracker barrel or its modern counterpart, the coffee cup.

Such criticisms have come from educators and laymen alike. Debates on education across this country have been concerned with whether school policies are to be determined on the basis of scientific evidence or by the whims of a vocal minority of the public. Some critics feel that educators have gone too far in complying with the requests of pressure groups; others feel that the public has been left out.

In order to discuss this issue and its implications, one must develop a frame of reference. Professional opinion is opinion based on informed judgment and includes that intellectual body of knowledge which has to do with the special skills and techniques educators must possess. It implies an understanding of the principles of learning, the techniques of teaching, and the group process; a mastery of subject areas; and a thorough knowledge of the objectives of public education. Public opinion, on the other hand, is the collective judgment of a given social group with regard to a belief or a notion that has not been conclusively proved and lacks the weight of carefully reasoned judgment. It reflects the consensus of the majority of any large group which takes under consideration some specific issue or collection of issues, and displays attitudes or expresses judgments concerning them at a given time. A sample of public opinion on any issue at a given time holds only for that time and condition.

Of the arguments in favor of giving greater weight to professional opinions than to public opinions, the following are the most prevalent:

1. Public opinion can be too easily swayed.

2. There are large areas of disagreement between public opinion and professional educators regarding what should be taught in the public schools.

3. Persons who oppose school spending are usually more

intense in their opinions than are persons who favor the expansion of educational services.

4. There are indications that pressure groups have forced decisions upon the school board and the public schools in regard to instruction as well as curriculum.

5. No lay citizen is as well qualified to make decisions concerning education as is the professionally trained person who has a wide background of experience and technical training.

6. Local control of schools through the use of public opinion may impede research.

7. Sound educational principles and practices are often compromised where public opinion plays a big role.

Arguments which favor giving greater weight to public opinion than to professional opinion in operating the schools include the following:

1. The opinions of students, parents, and other citizens are strong forces in shaping and influencing school policies.

2. Our democratic way of life demands that the public have a voice in making decisions which will affect the schools and the children who attend them.

3. The success of public education in our society has been achieved, to a large extent, through cooperation.

4. Since educators are usually more demanding than the general public concerning American education, public opinion should be used to offset this imbalance in thinking.

5. Securing data concerning what people think on a given issue or problem is basic to sound school administration.

6. To a large extent, the school depends for its moral and financial support upon the status of public opinion.

7. One of the most important techniques for the administrator is to know the community in terms of its groups. Public

opinion may reveal facts about groups that are otherwise hidden.

It is doubtful if either of these two positions could be proved conclusively. The education of our children is a joint effort of the public and educators working together, with clearly defined functions. The public has the privilege and the right to aid the professionals in formulating the purposes of the schools, and it should be provided an opportunity to do so. Teachers and administrators, however, should make decisions regarding the methods to be used in obtaining these objectives. When public opinion is heeded, it should represent that of an informed group. By the same token, when professional opinion is used to make choices and decisions, it must also be based upon something other than a personal bias. It is incumbent upon the professionals to take the leadership role and to identify issues and problems so that the public can arrive at an informed opinion about them.

Case Number Five illustrates how public opinion can sway school authorities and cause them to make changes in their school program and methods of instruction. Case Number Six exemplifies how public opinion can uncover facts about community groups that aid the administration of public education.

Case Number Five—Blackstone

Blackstone is a city of approximately 50,000 inhabitants. Its major industry is the processing of rubber and its by-products. An advisory committee to study the curriculum of Blackstone's public schools was appointed by the school board as a result of criticisms by a group of parents. A citizen group circulated petitions demanding that greater emphasis be placed upon mathematics, science, chemistry, and physics; that there be less use of audio-visual aids, more rote memory work, and more rigorous standards of promotion; and that courses in driver education, business arithmetic, and physical education be eliminated. With these criticisms in mind, the advisory committee was commissioned by the board of education to study the school program and its methods of instruction. The board selected a chairman, upon the recommendation of the superintendent, and the total committee was appointed by the board. It consisted of thirty-five parents whom the board thought would be somewhat representative of the school district.

The committee met every two weeks for two years. It heard experts from various fields explain desirable ways of instructing and of determining curriculum content. The advisory committee visited classes and teachers. The final report of the committee to the board recommended better discipline, less use of audio-visual materials, and the elimination of all core courses in high school. It further recommended that all high-school students be required to take two years of mathematics and three years of science and that the system of grading be changed to the old system of percentage grades. These recommendations were met with mixed feelings by the board. The board initiated some of the recommendations made by the group, but not the change in grading and the high-school science and mathematics requirements.

Case Number Six—Victory

Victory school district was composed of elementary schools which had grades one through eight. The village of Victory and its surrounding area were inhabited largely by persons who worked in a large city some five to ten miles distant. There was little production or wealth, but the community used the sale of goods and services to produce income. Its total school enrollment was over 2,000.

The parents in this community became very disturbed about reports in newspapers and magazines depicting the sad plight of American schools in regard to their teaching of science. This unusual interest in science came immediately after the Russians had orbited Sputnik I. Parents questioned elementary teachers about science. Two retired college-science teachers, who resided in the area, began circulating a petition asking for more science in the elementary schools and less playtime.

The more than 1,500 signatures on the petition started the board of education to thinking when the petition was received. The board selected three parents from each of the eight elementary schools and asked them to work with a committee of teachers, three from each elementary school, to help secure the opinions of parents concerning the needs of elementary pupils in science and physical education. Two consultants were employed for the study from the local state university, one in the area of science, the other in the area of physical education. The joint committee also used the advice and help of supervisors, principals, and other professionals in developing an instrument which would secure the opinion of parents about the issues at stake. A return of over 85 per cent indicated that the public was satisfied with the way science and physical education were being taught. Most parents favored some playtime for children and indicated that they did not believe in overemphasizing science out of fear of other countries. The committee felt that the community had spoken, and the members agreed to support the evidence found.

Questions for Discussion

Case Number One

1. Can you mention other ways in which parents could be brought into the classroom to learn about the school? Would this plan work in your school?

2. Did the parent-teacher association attempt to provide too much information at one time for the parents?

Case Number Two

3. Should parent-teacher associations adhere to the objectives of the national organization? Why?

4. What can an administrator or teacher do to help the parent-teacher association of a local school select activities that are appropriate for promoting better parent-teacher relationships?

Case Number Three

5. Can citizens learn about school policies through participation as members of lay advisory groups? What dangers are involved in the use of lay advisory committees?

6. What factors should be considered in the board's selection of lay advisory committees?

Case Number Four

7. In what way did the citizen group violate good procedures for lay participation? How could this have been prevented?

8. What action would you have taken had you been the principal?

Case Number Five

9. Should the school board have accepted the recommendations of the group which made the opinion study? Why?

10. Do you think the opinion study was valid?

11. What would you have done differently if you had been chairman of the board?

Case Number Six

12. Should the board of education and the superintendent have permitted such an opinion study?

13. What was gained as a result of this study?

14. Could this problem have been handled in another manner?

Selected Readings

Grinnell, J. E., and Young, Raymond J., *The School and the Community,* the Ronald Press Company, New York, 1955, Chap. 7.

Jones, James J., *An Analysis and Summary of the Significant Research Findings Concerning Some Problems of School-Community Relations,* unpublished doctor's dissertation, Indiana University, Bloomington, 1952, 246 pp.

Jones, James J., "The Principal and Public Relations," *Educational Administration and Supervision,* 41: 313–317, May, 1955.

Kindred, Leslie W., *School Public Relations,* Prentice-Hall, Inc., Englewood Cliffs, N.J., 1957, Chaps. 10, 11.

Lieberman, Myron, "Four Myths Cripple Our Schools," *The Nation,* 188: 179–182, February, 1959.

Lieberman, Myron, "Let Educators Run Our Schools," *The Nation,* 188: 206–209, March, 1959.

McClosky, Gordon, *Education and Public Understanding,* Harper and Brothers, New York, 1959, Chap. 11.

Miller, Van, editor, *Providing and Improving Administrative Leadership for America's Schools,* National Conference of Professors of Educational Administration, Bureau of Publications, Teachers College, Columbia University, New York, 1951.

Moehlman, Arthur B., and Von Zwoll, James A., *School Public Relations,* Appleton-Century-Crofts, Inc., New York, 1957, Chap. 20.

National Education Association, Research Division, "Public Opinion and Education," *Research Bulletin,* Vol. 36, No. 3, pp. 74–75, The Association, Washington, D.C., October, 1958.

National Society for the Study of Education, *Citizen Cooperation for Better Public Schools,* Fifty-third Yearbook of the NSSE, Pt. I, University of Chicago Press, Chicago, 1954.

Rope, Frederick T., *Opinion Conflict and School Support,* unpublished doctor's dissertation, Columbia University, New York, 1947.

GUIDELINES FOR IMPROVING
SCHOOL PUBLIC RELATIONS

9.

THE purpose of this chapter is to describe ways of helping professional people learn more about school-community problems and to help the public learn more about the schools. An effort is made to establish guidelines which will aid professionals and nonprofessionals alike in attempting to follow general principles that point the way to better school public relations.

Ways of Informing

The effectiveness of school public relations is determined in part by the media selected and the manner in which they are used. Selection must be based upon something more than availability. Wise selection of media requires that educators use the relationship between the basic objectives of the school public-relations program and the basic concept it wishes to advance. Appropriate media must be selected to interpret each element within the entire field of the school program and services. One medium, however, will seldom be enough to cover all aspects of a given problem. Generally, several media, aptly chosen to do a particular job, will achieve the purpose better than a single one. Public relations involves more than giving facts to the public about schools—it has to do with planning and working for good schools and is a two-way process. The media used should be those that help the community to understand thoroughly the nature and values of a sound educational program.

Summary of Guidelines

Few, if any, guidelines have been developed to help administrators, boards of education, faculties, and citizens avoid getting into difficult situations, and even fewer to assist them in getting out.

No claim is made that the guidelines presented below are a panacea for all the ills of the public-school system in America. They do, however, bring together in summary form, with some discussion, the basic guidelines found in research, experience, and case studies presented in this book. The use of these guidelines does not obviate the use of media other than those mentioned below.

The following guidelines are presented to help improve school public relations:

1. *School-board members should be elected by popular vote without regard to their religion, political affiliation, geographical representation, or profession.* Despite the fact that legislatures determine the method used to select school-board members, there is no regulation that forbids the people of a local school district from encouraging members of the legislature to work for legislation that would have the board members elected by popular vote. In addition, local citizen groups and others interested in improving school-board effectiveness should encourage the nomination of able candidates for school-board membership.

2. *For efficient operation, school boards should be composed of approximately five to seven members.* The size of a school board has much to do with its operational efficiency. When boards have less than five members, they find it difficult to do exhaustive study on problems of a controversial nature. Boards of education with more than seven members find it almost impossible to discover a convenient meeting time for all members. Also, there often is not enough time at meetings for all members to be heard on a given issue.

3. *Among the most successful school boards are those that develop and use written school-board policies and encourage their members to take part in state and national school-board meetings.* The boards composed of members who have a desire to learn and to help the superintendent are the most successful. Members of school boards who possess these qualifications often feel the need for written policies to guide them in board action and policy development. Boards that use written policies generally want to take part in local, state, and national school-board meetings. It is through these meetings that many boards learn how to develop and use written policies.

4. *The control of the school system is not the business of either the superintendent or the board of education acting alone, but is a cooperative venture.* The board is generally charged with legislative and judicial duties and the superintendent with administrative duties. This division of authority does not prevent their working together on many matters of mutual concern. In fact, it is doubtful if many of the policies made by school systems could be brought about without the cooperation of the board and the superintendent.

5. *With superintendents and other professional personnel providing essential information and advice about the school program, local boards of education should be able to make*

effective appraisals. It is recognized that board members are not generally authorities in education, but orientation and in-service training have helped to acquaint them with the schools and school problems. Board members, however, must constantly seek the advice and counsel of others, and should realize that they lack the technical training which the professional personnel may have. One of the complex duties of school boards is to appraise the program. They need all the help possible to make wise judgments on this important topic.

6. *School boards should spend public-school funds to become members of state and national school-board associations.* Every superintendent of schools should strongly recommend that his board of education join its state association and, through the state, the national school-board association. New board members, and in some cases experienced members too, need to be encouraged to take part in state and national school-board conferences. Part of this encouragement should be in the form of payment for housing, transportation, and meals for local members to attend state and national meetings. To do less than this is to deny board members the opportunity for growth.

7. *School-board members have many public-relations responsibilities both as a board and as individual board members.* Some of the functions which are related to its work as a board include: reports to the public, exchange of information and ideas with the superintendent, use of the professional staff in developing policies for the public-relations program, evaluation of public opinion, providing the means for interpretation, and orienting and educating new members. As an individual, a board member has no legal authority. His authority lies in providing the public with facts which are ready to be released.

He may explain policies and defend the actions of the school system.

8. *The person charged with the major responsibility for the public-relations program is the superintendent of schools.* He is responsible to the local board of education for all aspects of the total school program. Among the duties he should perform in administering the public-relations program are: organize the machinery for the public-relations program, provide leadership and inspiration to the faculties, discover and analyze outside demands and pressures, help to inform the board of education, and assist in evaluation of the public-relations program. Although the superintendent may not perform all these activities, it is his responsibility to delegate them or see that they are done.

9. *From the standpoint of effect upon education, school districts should be fiscally independent; that is, they should be organized so that the board of education has the legal right to levy taxes and to spend the income thus gathered without securing the approval of some governmental agency, such as the mayor or city council.* One may find good schools operating under fiscally independent or dependent school districts, but the group that has fiscal authority in determining the budget generally assumes responsibility for school policy. Good public relations are not likely to be developed when support for selected phases of the school program is not continuous. When school districts are fiscally independent, it is impossible to spend school funds for nonschool purposes.

10. *Although the property tax has many weaknesses and cannot continue to be the major source of local revenue, it should be kept, and its assessment practices and collection methods should be greatly improved.* Despite the wide variation in ratio from assessment to true value, and the large num-

ber of exemptions found today, the property tax should remain as a local source of revenue. The property tax usually provides some freedom for local school districts to spend above the state and federal minimum. It is the source of revenue most often used for local research and study. Additional research must be done to find other sources of revenue at the local level to supplement the property tax. The public often associates the property tax with local support and feels that it is helping to pay for the public schools through this source.

11. *It is doubtful if public education can provide a minimum program that is satisfactory for the increasing enrollments without expanded federal and state aid.* The great increases in public-school enrollments during the past decade have created financial problems of considerable magnitude. Funds are needed for instruction, plants, and equipment. If the voting public is desirous of federal aid without federal control, it must make a stronger request to Congress. As our nation becomes more urbanized, the migration of people will cause more communities to receive products of school systems of various other communities, and it will be even more important to have adequate financing. This can be done by taxing wealth wherever it is and distributing it to the areas where it is not.

12. *Spending of public funds for nonpublic schools remains a point of controversy in many states.* There has been little money expended from public-school funds for nonpublic schools, with the exception of money for the transportation of pupils, the providing of free textbooks, and, in some instances, health services. Despite recent discussions of the relationship of public education to nonpublic education, few issues in this area have been definitely settled. Even indirect aid to nonpublic schools is still a matter of controversy.

13. *Public-school funds should be spent for the purpose of supporting and improving school public-relations programs.* The need for keeping the public informed and sympathetic is recognized by successful businessmen and school administrators alike. Since so many school systems charge a part of the costs of public relations to various departments, it is difficult to estimate a percentage of the budget which should be set aside for this purpose. The cost for public relations will vary from year to year, depending upon the scope of the program and what the school system wishes to accomplish. Whatever the cost, the budget should include adequate funds for public relations so that effective use may be made of all the media that are helpful in telling the story of the school system.

14. *Citizens should be given the opportunity and be encouraged to participate in the planning of school buildings.* School-plant planning is a process that affects many people. If the best results are to be achieved, participation in planning the school buildings should include all those who will be affected by its construction—from the superintendent to the taxpayers. Citizens should take part in arriving at the general concept of what the community desires and should leave the technical aspects to professionals. Perhaps no group is better qualified to give information about selected aspects of the community than are its local citizens. All contacts that school personnel have with the community or members of the community have with the school personnel afford an opportunity for creating and continuing good public relations. School-plant planning is no exception.

15. *It is possible to design school buildings for community use as well as school use, without greatly increasing the cost, and thus promote school public relations through helping taxpayers become acquainted with their schools.* The taxpayer

who is well acquainted with his school is less likely to complain over a reasonable tax levy for school support. Citizens who visit and use school buildings regularly are apt to become interested in what the children do at school during the day. Citizens like to feel that their tax dollars are working for the community twelve months in the year rather than only the nine months when school is in session. Provision for the physical comfort of visitors does much to encourage them to visit and use the school buildings. Planning school buildings so that they may be used for public meetings and neighborhood group gatherings promotes good public relations.

16. *The first and primary use of the school plant and facilities must be for the public-school pupils.* School buildings and facilities should be open for the use of the general public during evenings and at times when the work of the pupils will not be disturbed. There must be rules and regulations if the community is to use the school plant without creating problems. The board of education should adopt written policies spelling out the conditions of use by the community, so that confusion and distrust will not contribute to poor public relations.

17. *School systems should have their employees make school repairs which they can do efficiently and have outside contractors do the repairs which cannot be done economically by the employees.* Each school system should study its own situation and needs before making a decision concerning who should make needed repairs. In many instances the local employees can make necessary repairs and make them when needed. In other instances the needed repairs may demand a higher degree of specialization than that held by the school employees, or the tools and equipment necessary for repairs may be too expensive to be purchased for one-time use.

18. *The real test that should be applied to the merit salary plan is whether the instructional program has been improved as a result of the merit salary schedule.* If some teachers are improved and others are reduced in their efficiency, then the school system may have to decide to what extent the merit principle is working for the benefit of pupils. Administrators and teachers should be alert, keep open minds, and do research to seek criteria other than total years of college training and total years of teaching experience as the determiners of salary schedules. If an acceptable plan for the evaluation of teaching is developed, it is reasonable to assume that it will have to be done by or with the aid of members of the teaching profession.

19. *There is a great need for in-service education for all employees, since teaching efficiency is not likely to remain static.* It is questionable if any professional educator today would suggest that anyone, irrespective of the degrees held, is in such an advanced stage of learning that he could not profit by some good in-service training. A teacher once prepared is not always prepared. Teachers who are happy in their work and recognize their need for professional growth tend to promote good public relations through the attitudes they display about the school in which they work.

20. *The effectiveness of in-service educational programs can be improved by use of new and better methods for evaluation of such programs.* There are numerous devices available for use in in-service educational programs, but the problem of evaluation is a stubborn one. If one looks for the purposes of in-service education and bases his appraisal upon how well the purposes are being fulfilled, there is room for considerable doubt as to the success of many programs which are listed by school systems as being effective. Often, teachers and administrators do not know what their respective roles are in an in-

service educational program. The limited objective instruments for measuring teacher improvement have added further to the problem. Many teachers have objected to being rated individually, thus making evaluation more difficult. The general public needs to be assured that its dollars spent in carrying out in-service educational programs are helping to improve teaching and learning conditions.

21. *A negative effect upon evaluation has been encouraged by the compulsory attendance of teachers at in-service educational programs for which they had little if any part in planning.* Almost everyone would agree that wide participation in in-service educational programs is desirable, but it is doubtful if forced participation produces fruitful results. If the teachers cannot be led to see the significance of the program, there is little likelihood that they will learn very much from being forced to attend. In fact, they may very well resent the program and feel that it is time wasted. Where attitudes of this type abound, it is to be expected that their evaluation will be negative. This feeling of being forced to participate against their desire may lead to other complications in internal and external administration.

22. *The main concern in developing an in-service educational program is the securing of the interest and enthusiasm of the teachers for the study of problems with which they are concerned.* Learning can develop and take place much better when it begins with problems of concern and interest to the learner. People who have a reason for study and growth are more interested and are apt to enjoy and contribute more to the program than are those who have no reason for study. It is better to use encouragement than force in such a program.

23. *Tenure for teachers helps to secure better teachers because it encourages a more careful selection of faculty.* This

assumes, of course, that a supply of applicants is available from which to choose. Furthermore, tenure helps to protect the teacher from unwarranted political attacks and reduces the fear of teachers that they will be dismissed without just cause. This type of job security helps teachers to do a better job of teaching, which is the foremost factor in school public relations.

24. *Public-school teachers should have a definite part in policy development.* A democratic leader is interested in bringing people together in order that they can work effectively and happily to achieve agreed-upon purposes. Group organization cannot be forced upon a collection of individuals; it must grow out of relationships of the people who compose it. If an administrator is to share policy development with teachers, they must be willing to accept the responsibility that accompanies their participation.

25. *The scope of the educational program should be based upon the purposes of education, a common core of knowledge, and the community feeling toward education.* This is not to say that individual needs or the needs of society are to be ignored. It implies that short-range and crash programs are to be avoided where possible. It is of paramount importance to have long-range purposes and to plan the scope of the program in terms of anticipated needs. The scope of the program should not be limited by conceding to whims of local people who cannot visualize long-range goals.

26. *The curriculum should be determined by professionals, with the aid of lay citizens, and within the framework of the state and local requirements.* Many people and numerous factors may be involved in curriculum planning. Our society is structured in such a way as to provide for cooperative planning between lay citizens and professional educators. School-board

members and pupils may also be included in curriculum study. If lay citizens participate in establishing what is to be taught, they are likely to accept and support the program they have helped to plan.

27. *The self-contained classroom in the elementary school has some advantages over the departmentalized one in terms of meeting total needs of individual children.* Despite the fact that the evidence is not conclusive, several factors suggest advantages for the self-contained classroom. Teachers get to know their pupils better. Teachers are able to correlate better the subjects within the grade, since they have the same pupils most of the day. This close contact helps the teacher to discover pupil weaknesses and strengths and to work toward student improvement in all subjects.

28. *The proponents of the comprehensive high school seem to have ample data to support their case.* This belief is based upon the idea that a part of the work of the secondary school is to develop those values desired by a free society. The concept is further dependent upon whether one believes that children of all social classes, economic levels, and occupational groups should attend school together. This position considers it wise to have pupils learn from each other as well as from teachers. Of course, much depends upon the basic purpose of a high school as accepted by the school and community.

29. *The method of grouping for instruction that is chosen for a particular school should be one that meets the needs of pupils, is understood by the faculty, has general acceptance by parents, and has a reasonable chance for success.* The primary purpose of any school is to teach children. To provide the best education possible under existing conditions is the major task of a public school. The purpose of grouping, regardless of which type is used, is to facilitate instruction. It may be neces-

sary for some schools to have a variety of instructional plans to do their job thoroughly. Research evidence in this area is inconclusive but does indicate that grouping should be done on the basis of what is best in a local situation.

30. *Administrative adjustments should be made whenever necessary to aid the grouping of pupils for instruction.* Where administrators are not prohibited by state laws or state-board-of-education policies, it may be desirable to make certain administrative changes in grouping for instruction. It should be remembered that no type of grouping can reduce, to any great degree, the range of differences within a class. It is possible to find a number of factors in which children may be alike, but members of this same group may be unlike in a large number of other factors.

31. *When homework is used in teaching pupils, it should be based upon school experiences and be of practical and useful value to the student.* Under no circumstance should homework be used for disciplinary purposes. It should be used to encourage independent study on the part of pupils. Homework can be of a type that helps parents to understand what the school is teaching. Homework should be an outgrowth of what happens within the classroom and not something to be done as a chore.

32. *When homework is assigned, it must be reasonable in terms of time and ability requirements and must not work undue hardships upon other members of the family.* One purpose of homework is to enable pupils to try out new ideas on their own, without the close supervision of a teacher. If parents replace teachers in supervising the work of pupils at home, then a part of the value of such activity for the pupil is lost. Teachers who make unreasonable assignments for pupils to do at home may be creating ill will toward the school. In addi-

tion, a burden may be placed on members of the pupil's family, who feel it is their duty to help the pupil at whatever cost to their own work or leisure activities.

33. *Homework is more helpful for pupils in the upper elementary grades and in high school than for pupils in the primary grades.* In the primary grades it is very difficult to get children to work independently. Their attention span in the first three grades is such that educational activities must be changed often. Children must be taught to study and to work independently. Homework should take on a wider use and greater meaning for pupils as they progress from grade to grade.

34. *Discipline based upon fear of punishment for offenses committed and having as its major purpose the prevention of disorder has many dangers.* This type of discipline is not conducive to good learning. It may keep the teacher from becoming aware of bad attitudes in her classroom. This concept of discipline does not locate the cause of undesirable behavior, nor does it seek to remove it.

35. *Discipline that assists the individual learner to grow from a state of great dependence to a point at which he accepts the responsibility for his own behavior or self-direction is very desirable.* Helping children to establish good habits of social living is desirable, whether in school or in life. To give this type of help to pupils demands that teachers use effective teaching procedures. Furthermore, it requires that teachers know and understand the pupils' behavior.

36. *Disciplinary measures should aim chiefly to modify undesirable social behavior rather than serve as punishment for an offense.* Reaction to misconduct should be of a type that inspires the pupil to do the right thing rather than one that seeks to restrain him from misconduct. Any disciplinary action

by teachers should be designed to bring about a redirection of behavior in the child and not to give vent to a teacher's own feelings. When a teacher discovers why a pupil commits an undesirable act and then helps him to remove the cause for such act, good pupil behavior is likely to result.

37. *Regardless of the system of marking and grading used, pupils and parents are entitled to know what the symbols mean and how they are derived.* This does not imply that pupils and parents should decide what grades are to be given or how the papers should be marked. It does imply that the school and its faculty should make sure that parents and pupils are familiar with the type of grading system being used. It places the burden of proper explanation for the grading system upon the school. Parents want their children to make the highest grades possible, which may cause them to place undue pressure on their children in a number of instances. It is the job of teachers to help parents understand that making high grades requires more than hard work.

38. *Before a faculty accepts any plan of promotion, it should be fully acquainted with the total effects of nonpromotion upon pupils.* This is not intended to suggest that there should be no failure in the public schools. The causes of failure are many, and some of them may be placed upon the school as well as the child. There is no known type of instruction that can make pupils arrive at the same achievement level in all areas at the same time. Nonpromotion is more likely to take place in the elementary than in the secondary school.

39. *The parent-teacher association offers a great potential for building school public relations if it recognizes that its function is advisory and if it allies itself with the national organization.* Parent-teacher-association units vary in their effectiveness from those that provide excellent support for public education

to those that oppose many of the things that schools are doing. Some parents belong to the parent-teacher association because they feel it is their responsibility, and others belong because of repeated requests on the part of their children. Many monthly programs lack quality. Some units have lost sight of the purposes of the association and do not realize that their function is advisory. A large number of parents have gained supplementary knowledge about the school through the association. Others are happy to be a part of a social institution that is helping with the development and growth of children. The PTA remains a great potential public-relations agent if used properly.

40. *Citizen advisory groups are desirable and can do much to aid public education.* Although the function of such a group is advisory, it can make suggestions to the legally constituted school officials. The citizen advisory committee has the advantage of bringing together many nonparents and parents whose children have already completed the local schools. Such a group of citizens can play an important role in the collection and synthesis of public opinion concerning school problems. This type of data can keep the school administrator from being overwhelmed by scattered bits of information from vocal minority groups. A citizen advisory committee can be a good medium for school public relations.

41. *It is most desirable for the administrator to know the patterns of organization and thinking of community groups.* Public opinion may reveal facts about groups. Although there are strong indications that pressure groups have forced decisions upon the school board and the public schools in regard to curriculum and instruction, securing data concerning what people think on a given issue or problem is basic to sound school administration.

42. *The education of our children in the public schools represents a joint effort of the public and the educators, with both groups working toward common goals and with the functions of each group clearly defined.* The public should help the professionals in developing the purposes of the school. The administrators and teachers should decide what methods should be used in fulfilling these purposes.

Application of Guidelines

The summary presented in this chapter should be used as guides to action rather than absolutes which are supposed to guarantee effective results. It would be helpful if the users of these principles could have insight into the field of education or at least a general acquaintance with its operation. It is anticipated that administrators, supervisors, teachers, laymen, and others who utilize these guidelines will desire to adjust them to their local needs and conditions. Through wise use of these guidelines, sound public-relations policies and practices may be developed or improved.